Poems to fall in love with life.

David Joseph Slack

Dear Son,

Remember you were born because of love,
take comfort in that knowing you'll always be
enough!

Get out and experience this world for all that it be,
see the beauty in everything,
be it a place, a person or a tree!

Share laughter and kindness with the people you
meet,
and know that bad people are just hurt living
through their grief!

Savour life's moments both the happy and the sad,
all experiences build character,
I love you,

Your Dad.

CONTENTS

1 Mental Health

2 Mindset

3 Values

4 Love & Connection

5 Nature's Medicine

POEMS FOR LIFE

INSPIRATIONS & ACKNOWLEDGMENTS.

My amazing Son Fran, for being my constant reminder that happiness exists in the present moment and to always be curious and wild just like a child.

My parents for always loving me, being there for me, teaching me that we have the power to heal ourselves with our own mind, and for showing me the beauty of spending time in nature.

My beautiful life partner Nel, for showing me true love and connection, on a mind, body and spiritual level.

Special mentions for the following for sharing their wisdom that has contributed massively to my healing journey….

The Chimp Paradox book by Dr Steve Peters,
Wim Hof,
Dr Joe Dispenza
Peter Crone
Michael Singer's book The Untethered Soul
Eckhart Tolle
Dr Jordan Peterson
The Daily Stoic book by Ryan Holliday.

The goal is not to teach, but to help you remember. Let these short poems and verses guide you along the path of self-remembrance, through understanding mental health to building a strong mindset. Experience the healing wisdom of nature in order to reclaim our wild roots, so we can unlearn what we've been taught in order to remember what we've always known.

1. MENTAL HEALTH

Invincible.

It's not about finding yourself, you are already
there,
It's about rediscovering and becoming aware!

Nobody can ever hurt me,
Everything is how I choose to perceive,
Circumstances are the facts,
about them I can choose what to believe!

No person can offend me,
they need my permission to do that,
So I'll always choose pity instead of calling them a
Prat!

It's not about escaping a place that causes you to
moan,
It's realizing inner peace will always be your true
home!

I am not my past, or what's happened to me, I'm
only this moment, so I'll always be free!

Enough.

Anxiety is like a pebble in your shoe,
It's uncomfortable but it's not part of you.

You can still compete in the marathon of life,
Wearing your past wounds without blaming the knife.

You don't have to work harder to give yourself worth,
You've always been worthy since the day of your birth.

How many more wins will it take, until people's love you'll
start to accept?
Don't let yourself go to the grave still feeling inept.

How much more pain do you have to endure,
For you to realize that it's you that's the cure?

Write a note to your previous self, and say you'll be loved
for more than your wealth.

Look back at your relationships from the past,
and be grateful even if they didn't last.

Give yourself permission to open your heart and receive,
You are always enough, now start to believe!

Stuff.

How much stuff will you need to acquire,
until your wanting of more will start to tire?

How many clothes will you have to buy,
to realize that beauty is not only seen by the eye?

How many followers or likes must you gain,
for you to choose happiness and dance in the rain?

How much money would you need in your wage,
for you to rip up the past and start a new page?

What's the amount of comparing that you must do,
In order to accept that your enoughness is decided
by you?

Compensate.

Are you an overachiever because deep down you feel
insecure?
You could look a million dollars, but your confidence is in
the sewer!
Do you work all hours, to avoid the work at home?
Relationships need fed, or you'll always feel alone.
Are you obsessed with winning to get approval from your
Dad?
Choosing to love yourself makes up for what you never
had.
Are you the constant joker, because inside you're falling
apart?
and laughter keeps a distance from having to open your
heart?
Do you buy cars so that others think you're cool,
because you lost all self-worth after being bullied at school?
Are you building a strong body to make up for strength of
mind?
Looking in the mirror for some happiness you'll never
find?
Maybe it's time to accept all parts of who we are,
What we once believed was darkness can be lit up by a star!

Intuitive.

Whatever you ask yourself, you already know,
maybe it's if you should stay or if you should go!

Your brain will overthink to avoid making a choice,
So ignore your mind and listen to your inner voice!

Life is too short to spend years in a rut,
Your thoughts will crave what's familiar, so always go with
your gut!

Society will give you a script of what you should want,
But you can use your own pen and decide your own font.

You don't have to live a life that's dictated by fear,
Just follow your intuition and your path will become clear!

Words.

Sometimes all it takes is the right words in the right order
for you to see life in a different way,
Poetry hits differently from sentences we use day to day,

You already have everything you'll ever need, so you can't
possibly have any use for greed.

Let go of loneliness, because you can never be alone once
you realize you have your own presence

You cannot be uncertain, because deep down you already
know,
When you sit in stillness the seed of awareness will start to
grow.

The more you force something the more you push it away,
So don't postpone your happiness by living in pain today.

Most of your problems you are the solution and the cause,
So release these illusions or they'll cause you internal wars.

People see life the way they see themselves too,
So it can't be your fault because it's never about you!

Life is never good nor bad, it's the description that we
choose,
Everything just is, so accept this and we cannot lose!

Comfortably numb.

Masking pains with pleasures, propping up life like a house
of cards,
The root is where your freedom is, not choosing easy
things over the hards.

We are all running away from some sort of hurt, if the pain
isn't obvious then the way we're living is the alert.

Society keeps us numb and not wanting to cry those tears,
but facing what you're avoiding is where you'll overcome
your fears.

With a variety of things to feel, always choosing pleasure
will lead to pain,
by sitting with what arises, there is always peace to gain.

Who am I?

Am I the name given to me at birth,
or is this just a label that carries no real worth?

Am I the thoughts going round in my head,
or the dreams I have when asleep in my bed?

Am I my face of which others see and know,
or am I something else, something deeper below?

Am I the job that I do every day,
or is this just a time filler that helps me get pay?

Maybe I'm the hobbies or what I post online,
but these seem too external and finite of time.

I believe I'm the energy which is boundless and free,
and I share this with everything from a human to a tree!

I am the conscious awareness that connects us all as one,
which will continue to live long after my body is gone!

The magic in my soul can't be seen by the eye,
It's a knowing that it's there like the stars in the sky.

If we think we are separate, we will destroy or divide,
So remember we are one then love cannot hide!

Enlightened.

On the starting blocks to enlightenment,
on the path you found through pain,
you now have hopes and dreams of living life a different way!

A few mile into the journey, your ego starts to descend,
people may begin to annoy you,
as negativity you no longer comprehend.

You then start to shed layers you've held on to since your youth,
and Society's plan is less important, as you follow your own truth!

You accept life as it happens, and don't resist what is now,
Your strength is more like water, you'll flow and simply allow.

The people who once annoyed,
you now see in a new light,
Compassion is what they need,
as they hurt from their past fight.

You've let go of all your labels, and the ego's identify to self,
You're feeling all of your emotions and you've never been in better
health.

Your gift is in your presence that you give to the world each day,
you now care more about love than what you receive in your pay.

You cease looking for an end goal,
for there's no destination to arrive,
Now deeply connected to the journey,
and you've never felt more alive!

Allow.

I've been having a few negative thoughts of late,
ones that repeat on a loop and then start to frustrate.

I felt unsettled and began to seek answers for why,
why me? I don't deserve this, not me, not I.

Before long all I could see was the bad,
I was so desperate to be happy I became fearful of the sad!

If something negative would arise I'd fight it or run away,
little did I know that would cause it to stay!

I got so exhausted I had to try something new,
these thoughts were just silly and weren't even true.

I decided not to avoid them, and just sit back and see,
I no longer resisted, and I started to feel free!

The Alchemist.

We evoke the world around us from the noises to a
smell,
we alchemize it all into a heaven or a hell.
We literally harness light to make the sky blue,
and our attitudes and assumptions will manifest as
true.
We are chemistry from the universe, what's in our
blood was once a star,
and our body carries ancestral wisdom from a time
only Gods know how far!
We are magick beyond our knowledge, can change
the physical with our mind,
and we can heal suffering in others by choosing to
be kind.
Any externals we face, we get to decide what's bad
or good,
and when life serves us pain, we'll grow like a lotus
from the mud.
The force of our own energy will never cease to
surprise,
We'll even outlive our body, because what's inside
us never dies!

Subconscious.

You don't know what you don't know,
Read that again, but this time slow!

Subconscious behaviors are hidden below,
We are blind to them, but they are still on show.

If we don't learn how the past shows in us today,
the future will be dictated, and we won't get a say!

Most of our patterns are installed before we reach 7,
It's our goal to learn from them before we reach heaven.

A life in autopilot will cause pain to ourselves and others,
So, find your own truth and stop living your Mother's.

Lots to experience, from people to travel,
all is made better the more subconscious we unravel.
Pay attention to our triggers so we can fully see them,
By feeling these emotions you'll unlock a life of true
freedom!

All for us!

Everything that happens is meant to happen this way,
Your body was keeping you safe when you had a panic
attack that day.

The relationship you sabotaged wasn't meeting your core
needs,
Or you didn't feel worthy receiving so many good deeds.

Those addictions you've got are numbing your pain, from
the root you're avoiding because you want to feel the same.

Take a breath when the body is sending signals of fear,
Don't hide under a mask or grab another beer!

We evolved to survive and to procreate,
so there's always a reason behind an increased heart rate.

Sit still now and then, don't always look for distraction,
You'll get a whisper from your intuition when you need to
take action.

Your body isn't the enemy, and your mind isn't always true,
Everything happens for a reason and it's always for you!

Addicted.

Addiction is the bandage for the hurt you feel each
day,
But unless you heal the root then the pain is here to
stay.
What we sit with and endure, there's no need to
avoid,
preventing yet another day of being hungover and
annoyed.
Once we remove the mask, the true feelings will
arise,
so however sad the emotions, there's no need to
disguise.
The heartache of loss or the sadness of grief,
Time is the better healer, than a bottle for quick
relief.
Each day is progress, from the yesterday you've
outgrew,
Addiction teaches us about pain,
that it's a tunnel you must go through!

Daily mantra.

Life isn't fair, nobody owes you anything, you are responsible for your own feelings, even if something happens outside of your control it is always your choice how you let it affect you.
Remember that somebody can only offend you with your permission.
Life isn't supposed to be too comfortable, predictable or easy, if it was, you'd eventually get sick of it and it would become a pain.
Life is uncertainty, so the sooner you get comfortable with the not knowing, the sooner you will have access to peace whenever you choose.
Life is about problem solving, not avoiding problems.
Remember that if everyone's problems were in a big bucket and you could choose any you wanted, you'd probably still pick out your own.
So, choose an attitude of acceptance and know that a life of no problems would only create its own, and overcoming adversity is what gives life meaning, purpose and builds up self-esteem.
Stress is not bad for our health, it is only how we react to it that causes it to be.
Small daily stresses are good for us, if we stress our body we grow, if we stress our mind, we are more robust and resilient.
Knowing life is hard will make us thrive and be able to find calmness among the storms.
It is only if we expect life to be easy that we begin to suffer. If you accept that things will go wrong but know you'll be fine anyway, that is the mark of a great mindset.
The more expectations you have the more you will get hurt.
The rain can only make you sad if you expected it to be sunny.
I will own this day whatever happens, and I will be grateful for the experiences in advance because I know that whatever life brings I can still find paradise in my own mind.

Heal.

We are all healing in some sort of way
Shedding layers of our past day by day.

Recognizing patterns that don't serve us after years of hurt,
Finding strength to let them go, and like a seed we can
grow from the dirt.

Healing is never complete, and it doesn't have to be,
each skin is a little lighter in the journey to becoming free.

With each new version of ourselves we accept the past was
still a vital part,
a necessary key to fully opening the heart.

As you breathe through each pain, your breath was once a
kitten's purr is now as a lion roars.
With awareness and love, you'll weather each storm
knowing the power is yours!

Daily reminder.

All of my mistakes of the past have made me who I am today, I regret none of them, I am proud of who I am and who I am becoming. All of the misjudgments, and bumps in the road were necessary, and I wouldn't be the person I am today without them.

Everything I need to feel I can feel from within myself, I don't need a relationship to help me feel positive things, I've got that covered. Relationships are about connecting with others selflessly and accepting how they flow without forcing anything.

You can't expect others to love you if you won't even love yourself, why would they do something that you wouldn't even do?

Intimacy is about deeply feeling the sensations within yourself so that you are able to feel close to another. The less connected you are to yourself then the further away you'll feel from others.

Have less fear, because whatever the future holds you are going to be ok.

You've lost jobs, failed relationships, cut people out of your life, felt uncontrollable uncertainty, and you are still here and thriving, everything happened exactly how it was meant to.

Peace is the result of retraining your mind to process life as it is instead of how you think it should be.

Peace is available to you anytime!

The Prison.

A millionaire who can't be present with his wife and kids
might be suffering the same
as a homeless man with not a penny to his name.

A bodybuilder with a back like a barn door,
may be weaker than a child who knows he doesn't need
more

A brain surgeon may hate their job more than a cleaner on
a subway train,
If your mind is a prison, then you'll always be in pain.

The man with the most possessions could be the poorest
of them all,
A second away from poverty if his house of cards should
fall.

The happiest of faces can have the saddest of eyes,
and the most obvious of truths can be the darkest of lies.

So much of life will defy what we see,
but that's just my opinion you don't have to agree!

The Recipe.

I discovered a recipe for a life worth living,
It starts with 2 eggs, one for less taking the other is more giving.
Whisk in some novelty to stimulate the mind,
so search the cupboards and see what you can find.
A free pour of kindness and create a bit of art,
now open up the oven and do the same for your heart.
Next you'll need patience and an icing of trust,
Now get 2 plates for sharing because connection is a must.

Changing man.

I'm not the man I used to be, I've changed in lots of ways,
Mentally, emotionally, not to mention a few more greys!
The past has many versions of me, but I've simply let them
go,
every mistake was necessary in order for me to grow.
I've lost things I thought I needed and found things I never
expected,
I now trust every path I'm on, even the ones where I'm
redirected.
I won't always go forwards, and things will take me by
surprise,
and even if I do go backwards, I'm still seeing the past
trough today's eyes!

The wheel.

It's not about reinventing a new wheel,
it's about remembering the one we have is already ideal.
Maybe just drink more water, or eat the foods you know
you should,
Or stick to your word when you said you would.
If you can't get stillness from your wandering mind,
Project energy outwards and do something kind.
The answers you seek are in the work you avoid,
So with lack of results, you can't be annoyed.
It's not very often you really need something more,
Most of the solutions are behind your own front door.

Spell binding.

The word Abracadabra means as I speak, I create,
So maybe think twice before using the word hate.
Words are spelled but they are also spells,
so let's cast them wisely to others and ourselves!
Maybe you're unlucky due to the words you always cast,
reaffirming a false story, you've believed from your past!
Perhaps you were told something runs in genes,
and kept speaking this thought without questioning what it
means.
Pick your own words and not those from your Mum,
What you repeat on a loop you will surely become.
You are not clumsy or anxious, you can choose a different
way,
Your own truth is waiting, and it starts with what you say!

Thought happens.

Thought is Inventional and it happens on its own,
Thinking is intentional, you'll see when you're alone.

Thought just happens, it can arise at any time,
Thinking is what we choose, feeding a thought into a twine.

Thought is creative, it can come from beyond your mind,
Thinking is a choice, like deciding to be kind.

Thoughts are more fleeting, they'll always come and go,
Thinking can be constant, like doing work with nothing to
show.

Feeling low is from thinking, from a thought we've chose
to attach,
the more negative thoughts we just let go, then less of them
will hatch.

Every time we observe a thought and accept it for what it
be,
peace will arise within us and remind us we are free!

The voice.

There's a voice inside my head that judges all I do,
It reminds me of past stories that aren't even true.

It says I'm not worthy of the love I receive from others,
and it keeps me up at night when I'm tucked up in my
covers.

It calls me an imposter when I try to make progress,
and compares me to everyone but I always come off as
less.

It portrays me as the victim whenever something goes
awry,
and it convinces me I'm a bad person even if that's a lie.

By just observing and detaching
the voice got quieter over time,
then peace soon arrived when I realized the voice wasn't
even mine.

Lockdown 2020.

A strange Coronavirus is circulating the air
A sign of the times as people start to care,

After the initial mad dash
and the bog roll panic buy,
people have gone within,
and slowed down their days
when they used to just fly!

Meaningful eye contact with neighbors
and clapping the Doctors and Nurses,
as we realize what's important
and stop seeking happiness from our purses!

Kindness, love, creativity and laughter,
we know the virus will pass,
but what lessons can we cherish for after!

You matter.

It starts with being present, not because it calms an overthinking mind, but because you owe it to yourself and others to be fully engaged in this miracle we call life. Don't treat others how they treat you, treat others with kindness no matter what, and those who are bad to us, shine your light even brighter in their presence and it might just inspire them to change. Don't have conditions for what you give, just give because it's the right thing to do, don't expect from others, just be open and show compassion to whatever path they are currently on and again shine brightly to help them see their way more clearly too. What you do matters, every single day! The brief conversation with the supermarket checkout person, the eye contact and acknowledging of the old man walking his dog, the phone call to Sky tv, it all matters more than you could imagine! One positive word can make someone's entire day! Let that sink in! Suddenly that person speaks to his wife and kids better, that kid has a better day at school, the old man feels less lonely. The world can be a dark place for many reasons, but we all have a light within us, and I believe it is our moral duty to shine it as brightly as possible, for ourselves and to light up the darkness for others too. My friend remembered something I told him last week and I felt overwhelmed that he'd cared enough to remember! What we do matters so much, we have meaning and purpose beyond words! Everything we put out there is our contribution towards making the world a better place, one person and meaningful conversation at a time!

This is me!

The word on people's lips is anxiety
but we suffer more in imagination than reality!

Many choosing acceptance over honesty
leaves people living lives thinking "it's not me!"

Be true to what you want to become free
don't be burdened by demands of society!

Humans need love, purpose and community,
so don't chase externals, be present and say,
"THIS IS ME!"

I can't, I can!

I can't change the weather,
the windy storms or rain!
I can choose how it affects me
and find beauty,
then whatever the weather is my gain!
I can't change how others behave,
I can choose kindness
and to not let negativity keep me as a slave!
I can't change what the government do or decide,
I can stay composed and see changes like the tide!
I can't expect everyone to like me or agree,
I can be true to myself
and be happy with what be!
I can't prevent all sad or negative emotions,
I can value their lessons,
allowing them to pass like waves in the oceans!
I can't change the world of its views or opinions,
or even my parents' stance of
"They know it all!"
I can choose love,
knowing I'll always be content
however the chips fall!

Inhale, Exhale!

Before you overthink any negative self-talk, take a deep
breath and go for a walk!

If the world is heavy and you're feeling a bit frail, gain calm
and assurance with a simple exhale.

When you're anxious and frustrated and have no willpower
left,
get back on top with a slow deep breath!

If people are annoying and make you want to shout, take 4
seconds in, then 4 seconds out!

When in the middle of a nightmare you'd soon rather leave,
remember how lucky we are to just to breathe!

Grateful.

I woke up this morning, in bedsheets of the softest cotton,
running water and a hot coffee, these privileges must not
be forgotten.

I have friends, loved ones, and I'm in good health,
Of course, I've got some problems, but millions would feel
lucky having a life like myself.

My job gives me purpose, I go to bed feeling fulfilled,
and a simple walk in nature can make a stressful day more
chilled.

It's always a blessing to be alive, whatever the weather or
mood,
So, get up, face the day and show some gratitude!

Note to self,

Remember that Happiness is a choice, it's not a condition of circumstances, I can decide to wake up feeling positively grateful each morning if I choose to, I don't have to go to work, I choose to, if something frustrates me, it's my choice that has allowed that. Any set of circumstances I find myself in, I can trace them back to my choice being the instigator or I can choose to work towards a new set of circumstances at any time! Responsibility is freedom from the chains of a victim mindset.
Remember that action comes before motivation not the other way around. Be wise enough to choose what I care about and what I don't and know that sometimes the powerful thing is actually just letting go.
I should be strong enough to pause and breathe before reacting, and not react impulsively therefore feeding any subconscious patterns that are no longer serving my benefit.
I shouldn't try to fix everything that comes into my life, but I should fix myself in such a way that whatever comes I will be fine with! I should let go of what's been and have a strong belief in myself that I can thrive in whatever the future holds!
I will accept that life isn't always fair, I will keep disappointments in perspective and realize that things come and go and challenges only help me to grow!
Paradise is not a place, it's a feeling! I can choose my thoughts as freely as a choose my clothes to wear each day!

Dear Overthinker,

You are not your thoughts, so don't let them define you! You are not an anxious person, you just feel anxious sometimes, you are not a worrier, you just get worried sometimes! You are the witness to the thoughts like clouds passing by, and the realization of this allows you to surrender to them without needing to try and stop anything. Like a puddle that's just been stepped in, your mind will settle on its own once left alone. Take comfort in the knowledge that an anxious mind is fixed on the future and a depressed mind is fixed on the past, so use your superpower by tapping into the present moment whenever you need it. Your breath is a great way to anchor you into the present; count 4 seconds in and 4 seconds out, and place your awareness on what you can see, feel, hear or smell in this moment. If you practice this you can train and increase your awareness like you'd train a muscle in the gym and soon you'll come to realize that there is a place of intelligence that is separate from the thinking mind, and all of the things that truly matter in life- Beauty, Love, Creativity, Joy and Inner peace, exist in this place beyond thought! Once you experience this for yourself, you'll be so hooked on chasing this inner bliss that you'll just laugh off any unwanted thoughts that do arise like unwelcome guests at your party.

Check your lenses.

If you choose to see the future through the lens of the past, then it may cause you to live in fear. The past has gone and all that is left now is the story that we choose to tell ourselves about it. Even if the past was harsh, we can still choose to see it through a positive lens and be grateful for the lessons it has brought us. By doing so, this can be the difference in us having more faith in the future and seeing it through the lens of hope instead of fear. By choosing to have a better relationship with our thoughts on the past, we can immediately have a more positive outlook on the future and more importantly be able to sit easier at peace in the now

Home sick.

Everything you want, quicker than you can blink,
Taking away our purpose, we don't even have to think,

Surrounded by people but still feeling alone,
You got an easy life, yet all you do is moan!

Too much comfort will only frustrate,
Not enough struggle creates a life you'll hate!

Seek out challenges and overcome fear,
You'll have more self-worth, and your anxious mind will
clear!

Taking responsibility doesn't mean it's your fault,
But having ownership will bring your worrying to a halt!

Home is a feeling, of being connected and fully alive,
So have time off your screen and don't be a slave to your
hard drive!

A fast-progressing world, with poorer mental health,
Money and status mean nothing, if you've lost connection
to yourself!

Self-talk.

You can be sad, but not depressed,
Not needing medication over a good rest!

You can be worried, without anxiety,
Sometimes feel trapped, but still know you are free!

Be in fear, but not be a scaredy-cat,
Need to lose weight but not call yourself fat!

We become what we say,
So don't write off a bad week if it was only one day!

Our words are important when it comes to our health,
So, think before you speak, especially to yourself!

Layers.

We all wear masks, it's easier that way,
keeping the distance between what we think and what we
actually say!

Above the soil presents as anxiety,
but the root below once seen will grow the tree!

We must look where we don't want to see,
in order to become free,
Don't delay the pain of today,
emotions need felt, they won't go away!

Our triggers are important, so don't ignore what they
reveal,
they point us in the direction of what we truly need to heal.

Our body will whisper signals to what we should explore,
So be grateful and don't choose to ignore!

We are all complex beings, with past traumas and fears,
but looking below the surface can give new perspective to
those tears!

Courage.

Courage to one person is climbing a mountain for the first time, to others it's going to the shop and avoiding the wine.

Being brave to one is jumping into the water, to the other it may be a difficult chat to a daughter!

One can be strong by lifting some heavy weight, Or by getting up early each day before 8!

Strength is not universal, its relative to the person, Comparing to others will make your mood worsen!

So take the first step, don't think, just do. each challenge is a brick towards building a new you!

Equanimity.

If we are constantly striving to be happy then it can leave a blind spot which makes it harder to stomach when things go wrong. Nothing is more certain in life than change. Of course, some people are luckier than others, get dealt a kinder hand, but at some point in life everyone will face the hardship of loss, death, trauma, job uncertainty, health fears, or some form of pain and suffering. If you are only able to be comfortable in moments of happiness or pleasure, then your world will crumble when faced with it's inevitable adversities. This is why it's good to practice testing your resolve on your own terms, so when things are harsh uncontrollably you are more resilient against the change. It's not sadistic to get comfortable with being uncomfortable, it's a perfectly rational thing to practice, and could potentially prevent a total meltdown at some point in your life.

The old saying of "if you kiss a frog in the morning your day can only get better" sounds silly but there's some truth to it. If we choose to face something fearful, we are creating a blueprint for our future selves that we can still be ok when life gets tough. Cold showers, 6am wake ups, necessary uncomfortable conversations with your partner or family instead of avoiding them, keeping your word to do something even when motivation has gone, these are all small versions of discomfort we can overcome on a regular basis, and when we do, we are building our mental strength and capacity to handle life's unpredictable tidal waves when they do come along. I believe as humans we aren't supposed to be constantly seeking pleasure and happiness, these moments are fleeting and short lived, and even pleasure can become less enjoyable if it's chased too often. However, overcoming fearful challenges gives a deep sense of fulfilment that way outlasts moments of happiness, and what better confidence booster is there than being able to back your future self to be ok whatever life brings, to be calm in the midst of chaos is surely a worthwhile goal to strive towards.

The light within.

You plant seeds every single day, with your thoughts, your words and your actions. We all have influence, much more than we can imagine. Everything that we put out into the world makes some small difference which can compound into something magnificent. A passing compliment that you nearly didn't say can lead to a husband being nicer to his wife as he greets her from work, a friendly smile can give hope to a stranger, a hug for just slightly longer can give a sense of safety and belonging to a partner, a positive text to a friend can ease their Monday blues, a hand signal and a smile as you let someone out of a junction can make someone's drive to work better, and the choosing of a positive thought on waking can change your own entire day! The world can be a dark place at times, but we all have a light within us and it's our choice to shine it and make the world just that little bit brighter! You matter, every day you are making an impact on the lives of others, if that isn't a good enough reason to jump out of bed each morning then I don't know what is!

Reflect.

Breathe, slow down, in fact no...Stop!
Reflect, be grateful and take stock!

Lives lost, too early and unplanned,
We detach and move on, but we must understand!

We've all been in grief, something taken or lost,
but unprocessed emotions will come at a cost!

Cherish the memories and laugh, remember the good and
smile!
Be grateful for the experience, even if it was just for a
while!

We still got to feel these beautiful things,
So let's remember to embrace whatever life brings!

Keeping busy and moving fast is what we expect,
But always make time to just stop, and reflect!

Pause.

I think it's important to check in with ourselves each day, notice how we feel, like we are checking in on someone we care about!
Ask yourself often: Am I observing the situation accurately or am I projecting how I feel onto what is happening? Remember that good decisions come from a calm mind, and we can measure the level of peace in our lives by how calm we are during the storms. We can pause at any moment and regain peace before reacting, and that is our superpower, because by doing that we can change the future! We shouldn't be too harsh on ourselves or overthink things when we don't feel in the best of moods, most of the time it can be solved by a decent night's sleep, drinking a bit more water or getting outside more. I think it's good to treat our mental well-being like an ongoing daily conversation with ourselves, telling yourself good things, absorbing positive material and setting up good daily habits. We can often take ourselves for granted and just fumble on through without giving ourselves or our thoughts the proper care and attention. We are all guilty of just living on autopilot, but by doing this we can get ourselves so bogged down in life's stresses when we could have prevented this with regular self-care. Try not to underestimate the simple things like breath work or 5 minutes of meditation each day in order to maintain a level of peace within you! Another really quick way to make you feel good is making a small list each day of things to tick off or having a good clear out of your wardrobe can work wonders! Life is just a series of small wins each day, and remember we are just the story we tell ourselves!

True Strength.

Today let's remember that true strength is simply pulling yourself out of bed on those dark miserable mornings when the world is against us, biting your tongue when you are feeling that inner frustration, choosing to smile when you are having a bad day or even week. Strength isn't always the all mighty presence, it is being like water and allowing things to flow, settle on their own and just like water finds its way through the cracks, you shall find a way through also!

Dear Jealousy,

The next time you feel a sense of jealousy towards someone, even if you know deep down that the imagine you see doesn't tell the full story, you still can't help a slight twinge of envy. Tell that person how good you think they are, this will instantly set you free from the chains of jealousy. Realize that even though social media isn't a true reflection of the truth, you are really only ever jealous of your unfulfilled self that is being reminded to you by the image. But if you do feel unfulfilled by looking at someone else's life, remember that every success has a trade off somewhere; Elon Musk is a Spaceship launching genius, but what's his love life like? David Beckham is gifted with unparalleled good looks, but does he feel anxious walking to the shop in case he gets mobbed? Always look at the whole picture and it's only a life worth feeling unfulfilled for if you'd be prepared to swap everything with them even the lows. Some of the most highly successful people on this planet may struggle to stay present with their kids, struggle with anxiety or not be able to appreciate something as simple as sitting by a waterfall.

Impermanence.

Is it just me or do the stars shine a little brighter this year? Are the trees more vibrant and does the ocean air feel all the more healing to the soul?
If this year has taught me anything it's that everything is temporary, all that we see before us will one day perish into insignificance. Change can come along in the blink of an eye, nothing is fixed! We like to cling to our jobs as a huge part of who we are, but we could easily do a 180 and train to be something different and still thrive! Our lifestyles: we can choose new hobbies, go to different places and grow with change! Our personality: we can wake up any day and let go of old patterns and become someone different. We do not have to be "worriers", "stress head's" or someone who can't play the guitar or rock climb! It's our life and we can reinvent it at any moment. We do not have to believe everything we hear off our parents, the news or our friends, we can live our own truth and still be loved! Even with love, we like to think we have to find "the one". The truth is there is millions of "ones" out there that you could fall in love with and still be as happy! We tend to let things define us and they become our identity that fuels our ego..."I am a vegan".."I am a rugby player" ..."I am a business man" I believe it's better to lose these roles that we give ourselves to feel validated in some way, and accept that we are quite simply the energy that we put out into the world, we are the presence that we give to ourselves and others, and when we start living like this we feel free and fluid like water, like we can surrender to the constant flows of life and be ok whatever happens! Things can be taken away from us at any time, if we've let them define us, then change will destroy us. We can still appreciate them, and accept them fleetingly like a flower that blooms but then decays to feed the soil! We can take courage from the lessons we've learnt this year, become unstoppable against our fears and have a strong belief that we could quite easily lose everything yet still survive and thrive again!

Hope.

Have you ever thought that if your life was absolutely perfect, with everything going as well as it could do, you would only create more problems yourself to get hung up about?
Think about when you've had something big going on in your life causing you stress, all the smaller issues suddenly fall into insignificance, but when you have no big problems going on the smaller issues fill up that space and seem bigger than they are.
The paradox of problems is that nobody wants them, but they actually help give our life some meaning, or to go a step further, hope!
Believe it or not we are actually wired to crave some balance of things being slightly fucked up so that our life still has meaning and hope.
Hope in its very nature implies that something has to be a bit wrong in order to have hope for something better. But It's not the something better that fulfils us, it's the hope itself.
A life without hope or meaning will soon lead to depression, because depression is not that your life sucks, it's a lack of hope towards something better. This explains how a millionaire, high flying yacht owner can still be depressed, because it doesn't matter how perfect your life is or looks, there is nothing more unfulfilled than someone who isn't permitted to prove themselves against some kind of adversity or problem. So, the next time you are wishing your problems away, realize that a life without problems, carries its own problems! (haha) and it's better to actually create meaning in the adversities, let yourself go through the washing machine of life, let the chaos come to you. Let it cleanse you!

Hidden Wisdom.

Being positive doesn't mean always walking with a smile,
Maybe it's being ok carrying sadness for few mile.

Being strong doesn't mean fighting off all the stress,
it can be finding stillness in among the mess.

Just because you love, doesn't mean you should keep,
It's better to let go if you'll finally get some sleep.

Sometimes the best message is the one that didn't get sent,
better a pause than something that wasn't meant.

The answers we need are not always what we've learnt,
Pain gives great wisdom, but the feeling is where it's
earned!

The inner child.

There's a child inside me that hurts more than I allow,
He whispers but I ignore him, yet when he shouts, I'm still
wondering how.
I can heal him through listening and giving him time to
speak,
and by showing the root cause forgiveness this doesn't
make me weak.
Our inner child is in pain because he's carrying all our past,
So offer him some kindness and the reassurance it will last.
He gets anxious around any partners as he thinks they
won't understand,
because the little boy inside requests love as his sole
demand.

Simply be.

When I can't seem to stop my racing mind,
I sit with my little dog, and I start to unwind,
He doesn't see past this moment as I look him in the eyes,
suddenly more stillness I'm gifted by surprise.
On the weeks I'm over stressed and my cup is about to
spill,
I head for the mountains and chase a bit of thrill.
My hands on rock as I pull up each ledge,
I'm connected to the now as I'm living on the edge.
If I can't pause before response and my ego is causing
alarm,
I dip in cold water, and I start to feel more calm.
We can create our own peace if we simply just Be,
By entering the body, we escape the mind, and we'll start to
feel free!

Joy.

To me, Joy feels like happiness is bursting out from every cell in my body and I'm overwhelmed by an uncontrollable urge to dance or sing.

Joy looks like my dog running freely on the open sands when the tide is out, and imagining feeling limitless with not a single worry weighing me down.

It is the calmness of mind that I get from being immersed in cold water, while swimming in a lake, gazing up at the backdrop of the beautiful mountains.

Joy is the sound of my Son laughing without restraint and experiencing the untamed energy of youth all over again.

It is the inner warmth I feel from connecting with someone, the flow of a deep conversation and that shared look of knowing between 2 people.

Joy is what I live for, what is Joy for you?

Addicted.

Addiction is the bandage for the hurt you feel each
day,
But unless you heal the root then the pain is here to
stay.
What we sit with and endure, there's no need to
avoid,
preventing yet another day of being hungover and
annoyed.
Once we remove the mask, the true feelings will
arise,
so however sad the emotions, there's no need to
disguise.
The heartache of loss or the sadness of grief,
Time is the better healer, than a bottle for quick
relief.
Each day is progress, from the yesterday you've
outgrew,
Addiction teaches us about pain,
that it's a tunnel you must go through!

The Balance.

You are not broken, you are a human being with unmet needs.
Anything you ever feel is in your favor to keep you safe. Your body
and mind are not against you, they are for you, always!
Any symptom you have is a whisper from your body to help you
regain balance in some area of your life, so pay attention to it and be
grateful for this message, it is helping you towards fulfilling your true
self.
Any self-sabotaging behaviors you have are your subconscious' way
of protecting you, because somewhere in your past you felt it unsafe
to show vulnerability and accept love.
But the truth is you always deserve to be loved, so let any old
patterns go and open yourself up to love, give it, receive it and see it
in everyone and everything, because love is the best medicine, and it
is better to see the world through the eyes of love than the eyes of
fear.
If you are feeling lost, disconnected, or just that something is out of
balance, check your social needs are being met; do you feel part of a
group and getting a sense of community? are you connecting with
others with real conversation? have you cultivated a sense of purpose
and meaning from your life? this can be done by contributing to the
lives of others, throwing yourself into a hobby or passion, creating a
morning or nightly routine to feel a sense of achievement and
overcome adversities to build up self-esteem.
Whatever you are feeling right now, deeply realize that this is exactly
how you are supposed to feel because your body is looking after you.
Remember that even with pain, it is beautiful that life always finds a
way to restore the balance.

Problem Solver.

A life of no problems will soon find its own,
We are wired to solve, be challenged and to grow!

A mind with no goals will look for silly things to hoard,
So, are you really anxious or are you just bored?

Make a list, set a mission, tick each day as a win,
You'll be too focused to notice that life might be grim!

Start off small, just run round the block,
There's potential inside you just need to unlock!

Try a new hobby or do jobs at home,
Most problems are born because you can't sit on your own.

With nothing to prove, you'll overthink your mind into a
circus,
So, choose your own problems and live a life with more
purpose!

Your Story.

Some carry the past wherever they go,
Like a seed never planted unable to grow!

The past in the present is just a story we tell,
So, frame it positively then there's no need to dwell.

An alcoholic Father shouldn't bring your life to a halt,
Because people have trauma and its not your fault.

The past relationship preventing you moving on,
Forgiveness I key, no matter who was wrong!

When the past causes fear, and its all take and no give,
Tell yourself a better story, for the opportunity to live!

Feel.

We spend time avoiding things that don't feel nice,
little do we know that in time we'll pay the price.

Every emotion is an energy that we must feel to move it
on,
What's blocked begins to hurt and the pain will never be
gone.

It's a universal lie that time is what will heal,
But things will only get better when you truly start to feel.

Witness what arises in the body, and detach from the
thoughts of the brain,
Feeling these sensations fully is the key to unlocking any
pain.

Our mind can be frantic and take us away from what is
true,
Find stillness in the body, and the present will be the gift of
a new you!

Nice Thoughts.

There's a song you haven't heard yet that you won't be able
to stop playing because you'll like it so much.
A person you're yet to meet that you'll never want to lose
touch.

A movie you'll rediscover that will bring back memories
from your teens,
A conversation with a mate that will remind you how much
their friendship means.

A takeaway after a hike that will just hit the spot, and
something unfortunate will make you appreciate all you've
got.

The most beautiful sunset is not too far away, and a
magical sunrise will start a future day.

Uncontrollable laughter and exciting new plans,
Exploring hidden gems far away in camper vans.

When you're having a rough ride or just feeling a bit blue,
Just remember some of your best days still lie ahead of you.

Self-enquiry.

What am I expecting from others that I won't give myself?
How can I take responsibility for my own mental health?
What have I achieved that was once a dream of the past?
but I'm now taking for granted because I moved on too
fast.
What could I savor more that I never fully enjoy?
If I'm never present, even a good life I'll destroy!
What part am I playing in my own demise?
and then not taking action by feeding myself lies.
Whenever we're feeling stuck it's because we're not
mentally free,
Then start by asking ourselves,
"How much of this is down to me?"

2. Mindset.

The bell curve.

The more we want peace the less of it we'll gain,
because it's only in the wanting that's causing you
the pain.

The more we try to impress the less of it we'll do,
because desperation is not the frequency of the real
you!

If we're always looking for light, we suppress what's
in the dark,
it's only by accepting our shadow that we prevent it
leaving a mark.

The more we know, the more we realize we don't
know,
So let's accept there's nothing to reach and there's
always room to grow.

The more we fight something the more we give it
power,
When we resist reality, we'll turn the sweet into the
sour!

Most things gets better until they get worse,
It's knowing when to stop that'll prevent a blessing
being a curse.

I am Love.

How we think, feel and behave creates our personality,
and through this lens we experience a personal reality.

If the inner voice is on repeat saying you're never good
enough,
no amount of money will ease your desire for more stuff.

If you don't like who you are, you'll attempt to change
what the one in the mirror sees,
or you'll get addicted to praise from others by living to
people please.

It's a superficial lack that makes us compare,
a job title, a bank balance or the style of someone's hair!

When we're living from truth everyone has the same worth,
we're all spiritual beings enjoying a short stay on earth.

Happiness is not about what you have, or even about what
you do,
It's more about who you're being that attracts the best life
to you!

We choose it all.

What if our subconscious is choosing the things
that we need to help us grow,
but because they cause us immense pain
it is keeping us out of the know!
Maybe it's in our contract to go through some deep
hurt,
So we can alchemize the suffering and blossom
through the dirt.
I believe there's a universal love that is always on
our side,
but it works in mysterious ways,
and it has lessons that it cannot hide.
Sometimes we feel like a victim,
but that's necessary too,
so in time we're able to look back and see how far
we've grew.
What if our past trauma becomes a blessing
someday,
and our healing helps many others experience the
world in a better way.

Always you.

What if nothing really has meaning other than what
we decide,
and how we choose comes from how we see
ourselves inside.
Everything could be neutral until we call it good or
bad,
a rainy day might be a nightmare if deep down you
feel sad.
But all weather can be fun if you're happy at your
core,
and any setback an opportunity for another open
door.
How we see the world is based on our projection,
and the lens we use to see it is formed on our inner
perception.
By changing how we look at things,
what we look at changes too,
because everything outside is a mirror reflecting
you!

The Delay.

The day we plant the tree is not the day we get the reward,
We can learn to love the wait and then we won't get bored.

When you always chase things
that you get right away,
You'll never have fulfilment that comes with the delay.

Constantly seeking pleasure is an ever-revolving door,
but a certain type of freedom comes with needing nothing
more.

Reading a book or learning a skill,
will build our character more than Instagram ever will.

Stick with a goal when motivation has waned,
Consistency is where lasting results are gained.

Most things are short lived that are given too fast,
so use the discipline of delay for a contentment that will
last

The gold.

The worst thing to happen to you, could end up being the
best,
Try not to dismiss that, just give it time to digest.

Life is happening for us, so stop making it about you,
and before you play the victim, check if it's really true!

Most things are just a feeling, that we decide are good or
bad,
It's only context that changes anxiety to something exciting
or sad!

All of our suffering arises from a thought,
we're attached to an expectation of something that ought.

Life will flow like waves and will continue to persist,
and we can surf with true freedom once we learn not to
resist.

Even the storms we'll survive, once we process any hurt,
Just allow yourself to sit and find the gold in the dirt!

Choices.

There's so many things for us to decide,
they can make us numb, close off or hide.

All of our choices don't need perfect precision,
the main thing is how we feel about that decision.

With endless options there's too much to choose,
So fully commit to one or you'll always lose.

We can be unsettled, even want something more,
but wondering "what if" will make your head sore!

Don't obsess over something perfect that you think
got away,
put energy into now and what's here today!

Trust yourself to make it work, don't worry about
the rest,
Most options are a winner if you make time to
invest!

Meaning.

They say Time is a good healer,
but Meaning is best,
It's the lessons we take,
If we see the past like a test.

Things may hurt us that we don't really
deserve,
but wisdom is the best dish that the pain will
serve.

By just relying on time, we may wait a while,
So listing all your lessons will give you reason
to smile.

Life will hurt, it's harsh but it's true,
but you'll always have the choice of what the
pain means to you!

How it should.

Everything happens exactly how it should!
It's only us that decides if it's a bad thing or a good.
Maybe you're sad, suicidal or depressed,
but then you'll look back on this from a life feeling
more blessed.
Maybe you're divorced, unemployed or been
rejected,
Or maybe a happier life is ahead because your train
tracks were redirected.
Maybe life's setbacks are just lessons that we need,
So that when our children get hurt, they don't have
to bleed.
So maybe we never have to regret or wish things
would…
and surrender to knowing it'll happen exactly how it
should!

The miracle.

You had to win a race against billions just to get
here,
Yet you still compare yourself to others and
constantly live in fear.

All of your ancestors had to meet exactly when they
did,
Yet you call yourself unlucky and throw strops like
a kid.

On Earth we are the perfect distance away from the
sun,
Anything else then we'd burn or freeze, and our
days would be done!

You are literally made from the same things as the
stars in the sky,
and your soul will live on long after your body will
die.

A simple fact check of the life you take for granted,
Will make every day a miracle and you'll start to feel
enchanted.

I couldn't give a f…

We wake up each day with a number of fucks
to give,
So choosing them wisely is the best way to
live,

Scrolling your phone to negativity and news,
Is totally your choice but several fucks you'll
lose,

Getting outdoors before any emails are sent,
Will set up your day and it's a fuck well spent.

Being stressed by externals will come at a cost,
so accept what you can't control or there's
more fucks lost.

As you assign your fucks daily make self-care
number one,
Don't run yourself to the ground because all
your fucks have gone!

The Seeker.

We seek the perfect body so that we feel attractive,
We seek marriage so that we feel loved,
We seek a job to feel that we that we have value,
We seek a house to feel secure,
We seek money to feel freedom,
We seek success to feel validated.
All of these things we are seeking in pursuit of a
feeling. With good intentions we seek, but every
now and then we must ask ourselves; How much
happiness am I sacrificing right now in pursuit of a
feeling, when I am more than capable of creating
that feeling within myself right now?
Things will always have their place and shouldn't be
completely renounced, but it's certainly worth a
thought of how much happiness are you missing
out on whilst chasing a feeling that you already have
access to!

Mastery.

Mastery doesn't believe, it knows.
It's the seed in the dark that grows.
Mastery is not thinking, but feeling.
It doesn't force and is patient with healing.
Mastery accepts, it does not resist,
It knows what it fights will always persist.
Mastery is not about being right, but about being free,
and observing instead of reacting to the things you see.
Mastery isn't separation it is connection,
It understands everyone's path is the right direction.
Mastery is learning to be instead of to do,
It listens to all but lives what's true.
It is choosing love instead of fear,
finding peace when chaos is near.
Mastery is the heart instead of the head,
and knowing the soul lives on when the body is dead.
Mastery doesn't shout, it just shines it's own light,
It doesn't compete with others about who's wrong or right.
Mastery isn't judgment it is holding space,
It is attracting and not having to chase.
It moves like water, taking everything in its flow,
A Master knows they're always the student with constant
room to grow.

You.

Nobody can beat you at being you.
You're unique to this universe and that's
100% true!
You can't see your own beauty the way others
may,
because you turn special to normal by
critiquing it every day.
You have no idea how much of your kindness
people still carry in their hearts,
so remember your worth as soon as each day
starts.
The gift you bring comes from your light
inside,
so shine without fear there's no reason to
hide.
You have a duty and a purpose that nobody
else can take,
You're a one-off expression of the universe
with a life you can choose what to make.

Nothing is important.

Before you judge this poem, think about what it means,
Your perspective is the difference between your nightmares
and your dreams.
Without nothing we can't have anything,
Once we've had nothing, we can appreciate everything.
When worrying we want nothing on our mind,
so we can relax and start to unwind.
We cannot see the magic in the night sky without the
vastness of nothing to contrast it with.
Our inability to sit doing nothing will cause problems to
arise,
Our brain would rather obsess or invent it's own lies.
It's only when we expect nothing that we can appreciate
the unknown,
So maybe try doing nothing instead of scrolling on your
phone.
Is it better to always be in need,
or to need nothing more?
I guess nothing is important,
so don't judge it's meaning before taking time to explore.

Believe.

It's as simple as this;
Your beliefs create your reality,
You can believe the best life and that's no fallacy.
What you believe to be true you will make true,
So what are you currently believing about you?
It starts by practicing a new thought,
not one you've had for years that was taught.
You maybe grew up in fear,
due to other's beliefs you let near.
You get to decide if the world is good or bad,
Or just love everyone because we're all a bit mad.
The more good you believe, the more you'll receive,
The more hate you choose to see, the less you'll be
free.
If you believe life is magic, you'll see it everywhere,
and you'll never be a victim feeling things are unfair.
Once you believe you will start to thrive,
and surrender to the miracle of being alive.

Embodiment.

Thinking will keep us safe, it is the job of our mind,
It's constantly scanning the world for any threats it may
find.

It will think up a problem that isn't even there,
to keep you vigilant and constantly aware.

In today's modern world we don't need repeating thoughts
to survive,
We can now enjoy the comforts of being alive.

Understanding this can help us detach,
before negative thoughts begin to hatch!

When we focus on presence we can be in the body and
away from the brain,
Instantly dissolving mental suffering or pain.

Your mind does amazing at what it's meant to do,
But by escaping your thoughts you'll connect to the real
you!

Perceptions.

We see others through a lens that we
perceive,
their actions will reflect what we choose
to believe!
You're always looking at a part of you,
so take nothing personal because
everyone else does it too!
We never see others we see our own
perception,
everyone is a mirror of our own
reflection.
So if we're looking at others yet it's us
that we find,
maybe it's best to always be loving and
kind!

Thanks Dad.

The best knowledge I've ever acquired is knowing
the Lake District like the back of my hand,
having the ability to take off in an instant without
having anything planned.
That you can enjoy simple things like a flask of tea
in nature more than a flash car,
because something matters more than what you do,
and that's the person that you are.
Having the discipline to avoid instant pleasure will
keep your mind sane,
You can experience paradise where you are without
needing to jump on a plane.
You'll always have everything you'll ever need, so
you can stop wanting more,
there is beauty in everything, that's what your
imagination is for!

Mother's teachings.

No matter what intelligence you hold in your
mind, it means nothing if you cannot be kind,
What you gain will not define how you live,
the most fulfilled life is measured by what you
give.
One small positive thought each morning can
change your entire day,
Seeing the affect you'll have by
complimenting a stranger will make you live
another way.
Don't dismiss the mystics just because they
talk a bit woo,
Open your mind to everything and then you'll
feel what is true!
See the best in everyone and keep an open
heart,
Kindness won't solve everything but it's the
best way to start.

The Unknown.

We spend our lives trying to know things so we can predict
the outcome,
but maybe there's a case for being comfortably numb.

Where the path forwards is only revealed when we begin to
walk,
and connection is better with less overthinking before we
talk.

Perhaps the future doesn't have to be set in stone,
and this moment is enough for us to own.

Where the road is a mystery and less visible,
we can predict less things of which we might be miserable.

How about we surrender and no longer need control,
throw your hands in the air and say "That's how things
roll"

Your inner wisdom can be the guide when you don't know
what comes next,
allowing infinite possibilities and nothing to expect.

When you choose to be at peace with the unknown you
can't be in a state of lack,
Trusting the universe will always have your back!

Placebo.

How you walk through a room is how you walk through
life,
Are you open to abundance or seeking ways to find strife?

Try being present and accepting towards joy,
Because if you play the victim, even the good luck you'll
destroy.

Thinking isn't only about being intelligent or thick,
Our thoughts start the chain towards being healthy or sick.

Repeat each morning with a positive mantra to say,
It will go deep within and change your entire day.

We can change how we see stress from something we have
to relieve,
It can be a challenge that we simply need to achieve.

So if you feel unlucky or think you may quit,
Maybe the life you seek is in the attitude you transmit.

Acceptance.

Accept the situation you find yourself in right now, accept it fully, no matter what it is, accept it as though you invited it through the door. We cannot move forwards, change or grow if we don't first accept what is right now. What we don't accept we are denying, and what we deny we are hiding from and refusing to feel, therefore we will never truly conquer what is if we don't feel it for all that it is and then allow it to pass through us and move on. There is a strength in accepting the current situation that liberates us to always be content right now and not shelve happiness for a later date.

There is no jealousy in acceptance, there is no lack or belittling ourselves in accepting how things are. Acceptance comes from a place of strength and brings an inner calmness that you can use to forge better decisions on. By accepting you become untouchably powerful yet soft enough to remain humble.

If you want a better life, you must first accept this one, but don't be surprised if your acceptance speech leads you to realizing that you already have all you could ever want!

Change.

Change is a fact, we all have to face
a constant flow, so it's best to embrace!

A flower forever in bloom
would lose its appeal,
change can be good
like the seasons each reveal!

Changes teach us to savor life's pleasures,
and care for those around us
loving them beyond measures!

Hold faith in the dark times
and don't make them personal to you,
Adversity makes us stronger
and the pain will pass too!

Responsibility.

If we think life happens to us
We're a victim plain to see!
If we believe life happens for us
the responsibility will set us free!

When things occur less than ideal
you can refuse to give your ego the steering wheel!

Accepting you are the cause and solution
of all that comes your way,
gives power and control needing no further excuses
or blame!

So next time you're cursing a problem or even make
that three,
take ownership and satisfaction by saying
"The buck stops with me!"

The Chimp.

That cheeky chimp inside your head
would like any hot person to be in your bed

When stuck in traffic it wants to rage,
if we don't take a breath and get on a calmer
page!

With every cookie we start to eat,
our ego chimp would binge and cheat!

Our ego isn't bad, in fact it's needed for
survival,
It just has to learn that not everyone is a lover
or a rival!

Take the middle path, no extreme will take us
far,
so take a moment after stimulus and don't let
your ego drive the car!

Play.

Laugh out loud, don't keep it hid, be silly and
curious just like a kid

Discover a passion, then ask ask ask, don't
keep your true self hidden under a mask

Don't consume more than you create, choose
love instead of hate

Smile at your neighbors and just be nice,
Milk the moment and lick the lid of life!

Stargaze, skinny dip and seize each day,
Learn song lyrics and dance more,
Let's start to see life as play!

Your Choice.

Two men are stuck in the same traffic jam, both with important meetings to get to. One of them feels enraged, "why is this happening to me!" "Poor me!" This inner stress stays with him all day, ends up ruining his meeting and on top of that he argues with his wife when he gets home.

The other man feels the initial dissatisfaction of the traffic, then takes a breath and realizes that nothing can be done. He then takes the opportunity to try and find calm among the chaos going on around him, which leads him to feeling a sense of enjoyment knowing he is surrendering to something he simply cannot control. He decides to put some music on and relax. This man enjoys the rest of his day, goes home and is present with his wife and kids.

Small examples of this happen daily in people's lives, now multiply that by 10 years, the first man is riddled with anxiety, chronic illness, finds it hard being present and is depressed. The 2nd man doesn't have zero problems, but lives life in harmony. Notice how I say harmony and not happiness. Life isn't about always being happy, it's about being at peace with whatever comes your way.

When an outside event goes against the grain of what we'd want to happen; traffic, a lockdown, your favorite picnic place is too crowded, rain on your wedding day, the event goes through a filter in our minds where we get to decide how we interpret it. So, the event itself does not cause stress, it is the way we see it that does. This can be said of everything in life; daily stresses, past trauma, future events, we always have a choice in what they mean and how we let them affect us.

So take back your power, realize that at your core you are untouchable, and be grateful in advance for whatever life brings. Surrender to it and go with the flow knowing you have and always will have everything inside you to thrive.

If you want to feel joy and you want to feel free, remember it's not what you look at it's what you choose to see!

No Regrets.

What if the worst thing to ever happen to you turned out to be the best?
Every moment you have ever been through, every decision you have ever made, every setback or success has got you to where you are today.
Every choice you have ever made was exactly what you wanted at the time, even if you have learnt since then and wouldn't choose it now, that decision has contributed to the wisdom you have and the person you are today.
Every failed relationship, job loss, broken bone, argument, panic attack or stressful event you have ever been through can be appreciated for the experiences they gave you while they lasted. Even when something good ends in a bad way, those good moments haven't been lost, and can still be enjoyed afterwards, like a great song on the radio but you lose signal near the end of the song, you still enjoyed the song while it was playing.
Every single moment you've had was necessary, it happened exactly how it was meant to in order to make you You!
Knowing this we can be grateful for all that's been and all that's to come and open our arms wide in order to fully accept life and cherish every single experience along the way!

Don't miss the boat.

Have you ever been so focused on looking for the nice
shiny answer that suits you best instead of doing the boring
basics you already know are right?
We shouldn't be too obsessed on which boat to take, that
we end up missing them all.
As the saying goes "there's many ways to skin a cat" So
best to pick one and adapt on the way rather than being too
selective and not doing anything!
There's a lot to be said about just taking any action, it
causes momentum and suddenly we find our way through
simply choosing a path and then working things out on the
way. The paradox of choice is when there is too much
choice that you get decision fatigue and end up doing none!
Ever scrolled through Netflix for 20 minutes and ended up
watching nothing? How about jumping from diet plan or
gym plan every few weeks and end up spinning your wheels
and getting nowhere? Feel a bit stifled in the cereal aisle in
Tesco? Ha, jokes aside, it's good to see how having too
much choice is affecting our lives, and check what we are
not achieving purely due to us flitting between decisions
and not having tunnel vision on one! Of course, it's easy to
get drawn in to the sexy new plan, the one the hot celebrity
talks about, or maybe you are just looking for ways to avoid
the simple boring things you know deep down are right.
Most people don't start for fear of getting everything
perfect, but sometimes it's better to jump out of the nest
and learn to fly on the way down!

Look from above.

Have you ever noticed how when someone cuts you up in traffic, they are immediately a complete arsehole, yet if we ever do the same it's because we are really late, and it had to be done? Or if you have a number of failed relationships, it's because you just attract dick heads? If we cheat on a diet, we immediately justify it that we deserve it! We all have these biases that we live by, and if they go unchecked you can end up living a life feeling like a victim or a snowflake. The key to preventing this is to stop and notice these little prejudices towards or against ourselves and rise above them by choosing to see things objectively, as a matter of fact, and that there's no hidden agenda attached. Sometimes things go in our favor, and sometimes you get a flat tyre, get caught in the rain or miss an important appointment. This doesn't mean that the world is against us or people are out to get us. Sometimes we may misinterpret someone's actions towards us, you don't know what troubles they are facing internally either, this doesn't mean that they hate us and want us to fail, but that's what we tell ourselves! If we attach a story to everything, then that causes us to write ourselves off as "I'm just an unlucky person" or "I'm just destined to be that way" which then causes us only to see the unlucky things in order to fit that story we've told ourselves already! It's a funny thing the way our mind works if we don't check it every now and then and choose to see things objectively instead of some over dramatized lie. You can give yourself a good chance of fortune in life by looking after your mental and physical health, but everything else is outside of your control, like waves in the ocean, sometimes they crash into rocks, and sometimes they trickle in slowly and dissolve in the sand. We are wired towards extremes, but we are neither snowflakes or victims, like anything in life, the truth is always somewhere in the middle.

The Becoming.

Don't be so obsessed with "improving" your life that you forget to "live" your life!

We are never going to know everything, in fact the more we learn the more we realize we don't know! I think it's good to get comfortable with lacking wisdom, be content not having whatever goal you are pursuing. This is not to promote laziness but to encourage being happy as things are now so that you are not just postponing your happiness for a goal date that may not even arrive.

Yes, it's nice to have goals, and feel that you are reaching a target, but realize that it's the "becoming" that is better than the "being". The end state will never be enough, you'll always have a longing inside for something else, something better, once you have the beach body, you'll find something that you aren't suited with and start another pursuit towards that. But accepting this is key; we are literally programmed to operate on some form of constant unease, dissatisfaction and some level of anxiety, because we wouldn't have evolved if we were just sat around happy as can be every day. Of course, have goals, but realize they are for the process itself and not the end target. Don't feel overwhelmed by all the knowledge you don't possess and get caught up in the state of lack that comes with constantly wanting to improve, you'll end up always hating who you are now and then when you do reach the goal you'll hate that too because you've practiced hating yourself so much. Be comfortable with who you are now, because after all you can only change when you accept who you are. But don't miss the bliss you possess in this moment while you seek the shiny treasures of tomorrow!

Today is an opportunity.

Let's try and see this day as an opportunity; when a task starts to feel heavy, recognize the dissatisfaction is a sign that you care, and realize that you can only do what's in front of you and anything else is outside of your control. If someone shows frustration, see it as a chance to practice patience, and a test for you to try and resolve a tricky situation and leave them feeling satisfied. If someone shows anger, try to frame their situation in a way that makes you feel love towards them instead of hate, we have no idea what battles people are fighting and even if they are just angry for no reason, it still has a better affect on you if you choose a loving feeling over hate. When we see the opportunities in each day like this, suddenly it becomes more like a game that we can take satisfaction from if we win each challenge. In that case, maybe it's not work after all, maybe its play! Have a playful day!

See it through.

A magic pill gives instant thrill
but no fulfilment like hard work will!
Easy come, easy go
but give things time and they shall grow!

Bite sized snippet, 10 second meme thing,
It's never enough to give a true meaning!
It's so easy to start when you feel motivation
but the greatest reward is the place beyond
temptation!

Short term fixes will leave you frustrated and
annoyed
because the lifetime treasure is in the hard work you
avoid!

We can all justify eating another biscuit,
But try seeing a task through when it's much easier
to quit!

Life is a dance.

Life is not a journey
with a destination in your head,

It's a dance and you'll enjoy each step,
if you realize this daily as you wake up
from your bed!

You don't dance to get somewhere,
you dance to enjoy the song,

and when you live each day in a dance
like play
you'll just smile knowing you can't go
wrong!

Breakthrough.

Lockdown or breakthrough,
Choose which you make true!
Old habits you've outgrew,
Make space for the new you!
When the world is uncertain,
and It's harder to open your curtain,
face what's ahead with love and not fear,
for acceptance is the place where
happiness lives near.
Open your heart and only truth will
show,
Whatever lies ahead is an opportunity to
grow!

Triggers.

We all get triggered from time to time,
but ask yourself if this feeling is really even mine?

Is that anger a belief of your own,
or something you heard when you were 7 from a parent
having a moan?

Is that envy really true, or maybe it leads to an
understanding deep inside you?

Look closer when something gets near,
is it what you want or just a learnt fear?

Discover yourself, and then speak your own voice,
Not one handed to you by somebody else's choice!

Lengthen then gap between stimulus and response if you
want to grow!
Recognize judgment as it arises, and then let it go!

Manifest.

If your life is stuck in neutral and you can't move
up a gear,
Are you motivated by love or held back by fear?

Don't keep denying what you wish to achieve,
Just put the past behind you and start to believe!

You are worthy of a life with joy every day,
So tell the story of yourself in a more positive way!

Don't belittle yourself, close off or hold back,
Have faith and be open for what you wish to
attract!

The life of your dreams might just fit like a glove,
So manifest it with belief and accept everything
with love!

Happiness.

Happiness is a state of mind available any day,
It's not a destination only achieved through
your pay!

It's nice to have possessions,
but their pleasure is a short stay.
The most lasting joy achieved is the one you
give away!

Experiences are the seeds for the garden of
your thought,
bringing a deep fulfilment more than anything
that's bought!

Happiness can't be reached or achieved in a
box of treats,
It's a realization of what you already have and
it's a theatre with unlimited seats!

Surrender.

True strength is choosing to accept instead of foolishly forcing something, choosing peace instead of being right to satisfy your ego, surrendering instead of naively fighting on. Flowing like water and not being rigid like a rock.
I believe we should learn to accept discomfort and uncertainty, and be at peace with them, and not just to tolerate them, but see them as valuable parts of our journey, we need them to live a purposeful and fulfilling life! You wouldn't want your child to have everything their own way and have a totally easy life. Adversity builds character, and an easy life will leave a yearning for something and a belief that something is missing. That something being challenge, opportunity to test ourselves, to grow, to overcome hardship and build a strong inner belief that we can be at peace through difficulties, so that we can fully embrace the goodness even more without an underlying nag that if this were to disappear at any moment, I may not be able to cope. Accepting what is and appreciating it all is a very healing lesson and one that can change your life! For you only start to truly live when you can confidently say "I will be fine whatever happens

The process.

Recently I'm realizing more and more to go into things just for the thing itself and not seeing it as a means to an end! We may look at reading a book "to gain knowledge" which immediately fixes your eyes on a goal and can take your attention away from actually enjoying the experience itself. I may look at walking my dog each day as something my dog requires and a chance to get my steps up and then miss out on actually experiencing the walk, being fully present for it, completely taking in all the sounds and scenery. It's the "thing itself" not the "end goal" that takes us to a place that really is beyond words, a place of pure peace where you forget time and get lost in the true beauty of being alive! Enjoy a conversation instead of seeing it as dick measuring against the other person on who can say the most interesting thing, be kind to someone purely for the act of being kind and not for the recognition afterwards! Love the process, not the end goal, then you'll be at ease all the way through the journey and see the ups and downs as all part of the same road.

The Good place.

Have you ever noticed when you are buying a new car, you suddenly start seeing that type of car everywhere? This is the confirmation bias that happens, the same as if you believe the world is negative, suddenly all you'll see is negativity everywhere! For every person who's tragically died, been robbed or had their dog stolen, somewhere else a child has defied the odds and survived cancer, a father has just learnt to walk again to play with his son, a whole town in Africa has just been given a clean water supply! We all know that the media promotes bad news because bad news sells, so therefore if you watch the news every day you could be forgiven for thinking the world is an evil place and everyone is out to get you, and not only that, you'll then eventually only see the bad in the world and in others. I genuinely believe the world is a good place, and people's default stance is a loving one. I think we are quick to assume the bad in people because it fits our expected narrative that the world is evil. I know there is bad out there, but if we look a little closer I feel that we'd see good in a lot more people and things. Behind every resting bitch face could be the warmest of hearts, behind the angry boss could be the softest of souls, behind the distant neighbor could be your next close friend! People just want to be loved, they just crave connection at their core, and often that longing is hidden by a mask that shouldn't be written off as "bad". Choose to see the good in people, they'll often act the better because of it.

Free Yourself.

Fear is a story of the past that we project onto the future which takes away our opportunity to change.
Often when we are hit by anxiety, it is because certain events can trigger us, bringing back a memory we have of a story we've told ourselves.
Grew up feeling inferior to a popular sister and now your inner voice says you aren't good enough? A spoilt only child and now you take everything personally and feel like a victim? Had an overbearing parent push you into competitions leading to a desire to prove yourself all the time? Bullied, dumped, sacked, whatever unfortunate event we've had in the past it can affect how we talk to ourselves today and rob us of our full potential!
We have all been molded by our past; through parents, relationships, school teachers, we will carry the stories of those experiences with us today.
No amount of dieting will work if deep down you don't feel worthy of the body you are striving for. No matter how ideal the partner is, your relationships will continue to fail if you don't feel worthy of love, you'll never be able to exceed at work if your inner voice is set to failure.
The important thing to remember is; the past is gone, so it's better to tell ourselves a more favorable story of it so we aren't impacted by it in a detrimental way today.
Our inner voice is dictated by these past events, it's deep rooted in our subconscious so it can be hard to change.
However, we can change how we listen to ourselves, and choose not to let these internal stories define us, and by practicing none attachment to them they actually lose their power over us.

We all deserve to be loved, purely by being here we are enough, and the story we've told ourselves that we aren't worthy is no truer than that of you deciding to tell yourself you are the most lovable person on the planet, both are purely made up stories!
When our anxiety is based on past stories we can often live in fear like a coiled spring ready to be triggered at any moment. This can be very demanding on our nervous system and make us feel run down, stressed and exhausted. By having practices in place we can soothe ourselves and prevent our nervous system from burning out.
Recognizing past stories that no longer serve us is key, building in a moment to breathe slowly when feeling triggered, spending time being present in nature and starting your day off with an empowered mantra is a great way to overcome your negative inner voice and calm an anxious mind.
Our past is not something we should look to blame people for either, these people are working with how they've been programmed to think and act, so compassion and empathy are better than the burden of blame!
Empower yourself today and change your future by changing your relationship to the past!
"I am enough, and I deserve to be loved, nothing can prevent me reaching my full potential!"

Good morning.

Today will be a good day!
I know this because I get the final say.

I'll get up with purpose and make my
bed,
my shower will wash away negative
thoughts from my head.

It's a new day so I've let yesterday go,
and I'm grateful for another chance to
grow.

I'll work hard and be productive, but
make time to relax and unwind,
to any people I meet I'll be present and
I'll be kind!

Good night.

As you close your eyes and rest your
head,
spare a moment to be grateful for your
warm cozy bed.

You'll feel so relaxed as you start to
breathe slow,
So start counting sheep as you let your
worries go.

You've had stresses today but now you
have none,
those 24 hours have been but now
gone.

I wish you dreams of happy memories
that you'll always want to keep,
as you drift to the land of nod for
another peaceful sleep.

What if.

What if you lose your job?
What if you find another?
What if that subtle change is the reason you find
your lover?

What if your adventure is rained off?
What if the news is bad?
What if this new direction leads to the best days
you've ever had?

What if you don't impress?
What if you run out of things to say?
What if these setbacks bring even more success
your way?

What if you trust the process?
What if you surrender to what be?
What if this acceptance is the reason to start to feel
free?

Embrace what comes.

Easy to be happy when all is going your
way,
But can you be at peace on a less than
ideal day?
The attempt to avoid stress is itself a
stressful task,
So lets embrace discomfort and don't
hide pain with a mask.
We can still be full without being
complete,
And praise ourselves with no need to
compete.
We can even move forwards in the times
we fail,
With setbacks come experience on how
to adjust our sail.
So don't delay your happiness until you
get something you desire,
By accept both light and dark, you'll even
find gratitude in a burst tyre!

If Thought was a Sport!

If Thought was a sport, how would you perform?
Would positivity help you win or is negativity your norm?

Would you think bad and make yourself feel blue, without
stopping to check if those thoughts are even true?

One happy thought at the start of each day, can make it a
good one whatever comes your way.

You can think yourself sick with a bad practice in your
mind,
So think twice and change the record to one that is kind.

We can walk through a world that's in pain or in trouble, by
controlling what's inside our own thought bubble.
Not everything around us has to be nice, we can still
experience the internal paradise.

Our thoughts can cause pains that cut like a knife,
So change your thoughts and you will change your life!

3. Values

Magnetise.

More effort doesn't mean more results,
Sometimes more is actually less,
If your house is tidy but your mind is a mess.
Too many friends but connected to none,
Money means nothing if your peace is gone.
When we always compete to get up another hill,
a constant pursuit to feel whole but nothing will fill.
The acceptance of enough removes the desire for
more,
You no longer have to grind yourself into the floor.
By knowing it's our vibe that creates our state,
We can wish love to all, even those who hate.
What's meant for us will not slip away,
no need to fight others to get the final say.
Happiness is less about what we have, and never
about what we do,
it's more about how we be that attracts the happy
life to you!

Heroes and Villains.

I'm a catastrophe and yet a masterpiece,
I am both the light and the dark.
I can be chaos and have order,
be flawless but leave a mark.
I'm courageous yet hold fear,
I'm a lone Wolf and want people near.
I'm both a Warrior and a worrier,
and a lover but I'll fight,
I'll stand my ground yet accept when I'm not right.
I'm both the night owl and the early bird,
I'm silent but you'll have my word.
I have a big ego yet know I'm nothing at all.
I enjoy the climb by loving the fall.
I'll compete and don't have to win,
I can be a hero and accept the villain within.

Joy.

To me, Joy feels like happiness is bursting out from every cell in my body and I'm overwhelmed by an uncontrollable urge to dance or sing.

Joy looks like my dog running freely on the open sands when the tide is out, and imagining feeling limitless with not a single worry weighing me down.

It is the calmness of mind that I get from being immersed in cold water, while swimming in a lake, gazing up at the backdrop of the beautiful mountains.

Joy is the sound of my Son laughing without restraint and experiencing the untamed energy of youth all over again.

It is the inner warmth I feel from connecting with someone, the flow of a deep conversation and that shared look of knowing between 2 people.

Joy is what I live for, what is Joy for you?

Acceptance.

Accept the situation you find yourself in right now, accept it fully, no matter what it is, accept it as though you invited it through the door. We cannot move forwards, change or grow if we don't first accept what is right now. What we don't accept we are denying, and what we deny we are hiding from and refusing to feel, therefore we will never truly conquer what is if we don't feel it for all that it is and then allow it to pass through us and move on. There is a strength in accepting the current situation that liberates us to always be content right now and not shelve happiness for a later date.

There is no jealousy in acceptance, there is no lack or belittling ourselves in accepting how things are. Acceptance comes from a place of strength and brings an inner calmness that you can use to forge better decisions on. By accepting you become untouchably powerful yet soft enough to remain humble.

If you want a better life you must first accept this one, but don't be surprised if your acceptance speech leads you to realising that you already have all you could ever want!

Talk to me.

Let's talk about the placebo affect not crypto. Let's discuss
attachment style instead of Twitter.
How about a chat on love languages not Love Island! Tell
me your favourite quote or poem not how many followers
you've got!
Tell me about the Vikings or some cool dinosaur facts.
Evolutionary Psychology not Kim Kardashian's breakup!
David Attenborough instead of Piers Morgan! Let's get
educated on Masculine/Feminine energy and tantra, not
office gossip and corrupt politicians!
Opening our 3rd eye's intuition instead of conspiracy
theories! Authentic connection instead of choosing a side
to be on!
Let's make healing from past traumas trendy, can't
vulnerability and owning our awkwardness be popular?
Tell me what you are you manifesting, not how much you
hate your job!
Let's discuss love to end war, that's what transcending our
ego is for!
Not everything has to be sexy or cute!
How about integrating our shadow sides or getting back to
our roots?
We might lose people for having a complex mind,
but when your vibe attracts your tribe, you'll have an
unbreakable bind!

Personal vow.

I will Love myself enough to not believe
the projections of others,
I will trust my gut feeling to know my
own truth from another's
I'll practice the awareness to not let my
ego get in the way,
and I'll focus on the present to enjoy
what's here today.
I'll show compassion to all whatever path
they're on,
and I'll keep loving in my heart no matter
who's right or wrong.

The opposite way.

Maybe you don't need to compete or beat the rest, maybe
you'd be happier not being the best.

How about not avoiding stress or fear,
and accepting they are part of life and will always be near.

Try not expecting things to go right,
you may be having the best day and then step in some
shite!

Treat anxiety as though you invited it through the door,
and welcome uncertainty without needing to know more!

Nobody is owed a life without pain,
so embracing that thought could make you dance in the
rain!

Get comfortable knowing change is always on the way,
it will make you more present and enjoy every day!

Watch your words.

We all love a gossip, it's how we are wired,
but negativity and drama can make us all tired.

The words we say change who we are,
so saying something positive will make you
shine like a star!

It's a chain of thoughts, actions and habits to
make our personality,
so think before you speak and remember who
you want to be!

Try saying something kind, compliment or
praise,
It could make a big difference and give life to
people's days!

Go without.

A lot gets said on what we need,
but in the not having we can heal from any
greed!

Easy to chase the flame of your want or
desire,
but when you appreciate what you have you'll
start an everlasting fire!

Always seeking more puts you in a constant
state of lack,
So make now your priority before looking
forward or back!

It's good to set goals or aim for something
nice,
Just remember before you start, you must be
willing to sacrifice!

The Every day.

I heard it described recently how the level of detail they put into the trash cans at Disney World is insane! Each area having its own uniquely designed bin to heighten the experience of being there. Stay with me here; it's so easy to only focus on the big things in life, the Space Mountains, the huge attractions, the summer holidays, or the weekends away! But most of our life is spent doing the normal, day to day, mundane things. So surely a better life would be to really dial down on these, pay extra attention to them, and let the big things take care of themselves! Think how many times over the course of a lifetime you're going to greet your loved one at the door, pick up your Son, say "Good morning" to your work colleagues or even do your own morning routine for that matter! If I've learned anything this past year it's to fully enjoy the little mundane things, because they are the ever presents and the easy wins to get right each day and also make a regular positive impact on the lives of others. So, be the most enthusiastic greeter in the mornings, hug your partner tighter than necessary after work, be overly silly with your Son when picking him up, look up and smile when someone enters the room, and the next time you circle an "important" date in your calendar, why not get a really nice pen you enjoy writing with, after all it's something you are likely to use every day, and every day is special, right?

Like Yourself.

I believe the highest form of unhappiness is not liking ourselves. The two main reasons for not liking ourselves are; We are carrying shame or guilt due to some actions in the past we aren't proud of, this creates a subconscious story in our head that we are a bad person and therefore don't deserve to be happy. Or, we may not like ourselves due to false impressions we have picked up based on how others have treated us, therefore we wrongly conclude we are bad and don't deserve to be happy. Firstly, nobody is perfect, we are all capable of cruel acts, and doing things we aren't proud of. But we can make a choice to do better moving forwards and let the past story of ourselves go. We should also realise that other people's actions towards us are a reflection of them and their own disliking of themselves and nothing to do with us, therefore we must not allow their actions to decrease our own self-worth.
So, once we've removed the "disliking" of ourselves, what can we do to start "liking"ourselves?
A lot of self-worth is built up from feeling like we are part of a community, and not only that, but believing that we are contributing positively to it. Feeling part of something is one of the highest forms of happiness because it's giving us a purpose to be here, it leads to connecting with others and therefore adding worth to other people's lives!
So in a nutshell- we like ourselves more if we let the past go, feel like we are part of a community and add value to the lives of others.
Does unconditional kindness sound like a good place to start?

Truth.

I'm realising more and more how important it is to tell the truth, to others and also ourselves!
Being dishonest or lying about something might be easier for us when there is some pain waiting for us behind the truth, but by being dishonest we are purely just delaying and also increasing the pain.
I believe that our conscience keeps the score and every time we are dishonest, it may be ok initially but in time it will attempt to level things up through our subconscious behaviour. This can come about by behaviours such as self-sabotage, which means we will subliminally ruin circumstances that we believe deep down we don't deserve.
I believe that we can only connect with others as deeply as we are connected to our true selves. We may have to face our darkest shadows, accept them and decide to let them go in order to live a life of truth. But forgiveness and the decision to live your truth are powers always available to us!
The truth is effortless, it is just exactly as the chips fall, dishonesty is energy draining, it demands a lot to maintain it and eventually catches up to us.
The distance that you are from your true self is the distance you will feel from others. We all have an inner voice that will always know the truth if we listen to it.
The truth is freedom to live a happier life for yourself and for others, because when we change ourselves we also change the world.

Follow your passions.

You could rescue an old lady from a burning building and still someone somewhere would say you're a prick!
No matter what you do you'll never please everyone, so it's best to be true to yourself and have fun doing what you love. Whether that's running barefoot or collecting stamps, you don't have to fit the mould that society hands out! Remember that your random, uniqueness and weirdness are what set you apart from others and are your biggest assets, so use them to your advantage!
You may as well take a risk on something you are passionate about because you could end up failing as something you don't like!

Wholeheartedly.

I think the art of living is to wholeheartedly feel things. That morning coffee, really savour it and smile to yourself as you take each sip! Looking out of the window on a rainy day, watching the leaves blow past and basking in a bit of people watching in their hurried states! Listening to your favourite band and the anticipation of reaching a really good bit in a song, getting lost in an epic movie and then sharing the enjoyment of discussing it with someone afterwards! Sunshine or rain, there are countless magical moments at our fingertips, and it is beyond a miracle to be here and experience the absolute beautiful mundaneness of daily life!

Minimalism.

Modern society pressures us into seeking quick satisfaction from externals and needing more. The very core of advertising is to make us feel low so that we need their product to feel high! The reason you see more adverts in the Sunday papers is because statistically people are feeling lower on a Sunday at the thought of the weekend being over!
We are less vulnerable to the pressures of society when we have more self-worth and an understanding that true happiness can only come from within ourselves.
By getting out in nature, being grateful for what we have, needing less, being kind to others and embracing life's struggles as a good thing, we will have purpose, meaning and fulfilment, the perfect cocktail to sit with in our own company and feel pure bliss!

Presence.

Let's be present and see what we feel,
any hurt that's inside us will instantly heal!

Hold on to no pain, a bad day or a row,
be still in the moment and appreciate what's
now!

A lot can be seen by slowing our minds
hamster wheel,
the surroundings of nature are suddenly more
real!

Don't miss these moments from the gifts of
the present,
make this a habit and everything you feel is
pleasant!

Be aware, pay attention, this life is your lot
Make love to the moment and live now
because that's all you've got!

Book the flights.

Take the risk, book the tickets, and do
not hide,
living a cautious life is just a slow suicide!

Climb the rock, make the call, better to
have lots on your life's highlights wall!

Most people regret what they did not do,
and I doubt many look back at mistakes
saying they have not grew!

Life is too short to not have cream on
your scone, so let's skinny dip in the sea
coz you'll blink and we're gone!

Fleeting moments.

Nothing lasts forever, but that's ok, we need
the dark nights so we can appreciate the day!

An endless summer would only cause pain, so
let's all be thankful next time it starts to rain.

Don't seek more, just accept what comes,
like a river flows and nourishes as it runs

Kiss life's joys and then let them fly, we can
enjoy living more knowing one day we'll die!

Small pleasures.

That beautiful smell of freshly cut
grass,
watching the rain from your window,
enjoying the sound as it hits the glass!
Getting lost in a really good song, or
knowing your favourite movie is
about to come on!
Chatting to a friend and realising the
same thing you were both about to
say,
or that pleasant exhaustion after a
productive day!
Learning a new word and using it in a
sentence, a morning coffee or the
shape of a cloud!
These are the little things, but let's
praise them loud!

Want to want?

It's not what you want in life, it's what you "want" to want that really matters! Think about that carefully. Most of our impulsive wants in life are driven by our parents, social circles, Instagram, or the news. We have to look beyond our influences to know what we really want in life. Growing up following the footsteps of others is great if that's what feels true to you, but ask yourself if you are really just choosing acceptance over honesty, would you rather live a more adventurous life that feels more in line with your true self? Are you wearing a mask to fit a mould that you think someone else wants? Life is too precious to not live in a way that is true to yourself, even if it means removing people from your life. It's better to breathe in the air of solitude than to suffocate to death in a crowd.

Inspiration.

Inspiration is everywhere,
from a poster on a wall to someone cutting your hair!

From athletes to movie stars,
to celebs off Instagram who drive flash cars!

The cleaner at work, who takes pride in her job, or the man
in the street you pass walking his dog!

A close friend who's having a rough ride, could help you
see you've got more strength inside!

A tiny change in habits or health, can lead towards you
inspiring yourself!

See each day as a test, a new opportunity to grow,
You'll soon be an unstoppable train that once started off
slow!

By showing up each day and choosing not to hide,
is an inspiration to others and should fill you with pride!

Inspiration is all around us, but don't just take it from me,
Remember it's not what you look at it's what you choose to
see!

Smooth operator.

We can often praise relentless drive,
the never say die approach to being alive!

Competition and money fuel the ego,
Making you a slave to working and watching
things grow!

It's ok to stop, relax and be still,
Instead of always grinding to get up the hill

Learn to sit and just appreciate what's around,
before you burnout, or run yourself into the
ground!

Reckless movement will not last,
So move slow to move smooth,
and move smooth to move fast!

Listen carefully.

Everyone we meet can amaze us in some way,
so lets really listen to what they have to say.

We all have something unique to share,
so maybe paying attention is the best way to care.

We hear more when we are truly present,
Instead of just smiling so they think we're pleasant.

In a real conversation there's no need to compete,
so stop trying to impress and just let people speak.

Not all encounters are about what you can get,
just engage in a chat that you won't instantly forget.

Your image and words might attract you a lover,
but only true presence will connect you to each
other.

Materials and status make people follow us or
hound us,
but nothing is more important than how we relate
to those around us.

The Basics.

I can't pinpoint when, but at some point in my life I started to deeply love the small basic things, that I imagine many may take for granted. Things such as having a nice warm shower I actually really look forward to and am not ashamed to say is one of the highlights in my day.

Sitting in silence with a hot coffee in my favourite cup is truly blissful to me, and feeling the soft duvet against my skin is up there with anything I've ever experienced.

At first thought you may think this sounds like a boring life if those mundane activities I hold in such high regard. To that, I'd like to say that I'm no Christopher Columbus, but I have travelled to exotic places, seen jaw dropping landscapes, chased the hedonic treadmill of pleasure seeking, and pushed my body to its limits, yet the basic things in life have never lost their appeal to me.

It started to dawn on me recently, that because of my love of these simple things, I honestly can't remember the last time I've had a bad day. Of course I experience bad moments within my days, but I know that I'm always going to have things that fill my heart with joy every day, and it's possibly due to the hardships I have had that has allowed me to savour the simple things so much too.

I'm not writing this to boast of the happy life I have, it's purely an attempt to share my experience of living so that it may help others in some way.

I hope the next time you are sat in silence with a cuppa, having a warm shower or snuggled up in your soft duvet, you realise that millions of people would give anything to enjoy these privileges, so savour them, prolong them, milk the fuck out of them, because life is too short to just live in autopilot, look forward to "the big things" and then die.

Algorithm.

Social media is a democracy that gives us more of what we
like,
But we look through the eyes of pleasure, so what we see
isn't always right.

With awareness we can step back,
and make up our own mind,
Feeling a trigger of jealousy,
but still choosing to be kind.

With feeds full of 6 packs, or girls of near perfection,
our desires will be shallow and we'll struggle to find
connection.

If we're careful what we fill
our subconscious minds with each day,
we can maintain our true values
before an algorithm takes them away.

So before we count our followers
or scroll while we're daydreaming,
remember you're a human
who needs a life with meaning.

…and a Happy New Year!

In this new 365 day trip around the sun,
I will see life like a child by keeping things playful and fun.

I'll seek balance between accepting what is and striving for more,
and know with any failure I can pick myself off the floor.

I'll realise my power and what I can control,
or when I need to surrender and say "that's how things roll"

I'll be grateful for everything, including the past,
and understand when I'm low, that sad times don't last.

I will stay curious and open and not set in my ways,
and have a deep-rooted purpose to bring life to people's days.

I'll chase experiences and keep adventure in my heart,
and value the process not the end in any goal that I start.

I will recognise the subconscious layers that I still need to shed,
and I won't become attached to anxious thoughts in my head.

I'll show up my best for others by prioritising self-care,
and I'll embrace my imperfections like wrinkles or grey hair.

I will choose faith in what could be, instead of fear of what might,
and I'll see beauty in simple things like stargazing at night.

But my most important task as I rise each morning from my covers,
is to bring a presence to the world and share a connection with
others.

4. Love & Connection

Safety first.

I used to tolerate a lot in life because I was eager to please,
I thought putting others before me would help me live with
ease.

I didn't want to lose people or hurt them in any way,
so I'd suffer in silence because I never knew what to say.

Then I realized I can love with boundaries and keep myself
safe as well,
so everyone gets the best of me, knowing the truth I'll
always tell.

If we don't protect ourselves from the pain of self-
abandonment,
we'll burnout and aim frustration at the loved ones we now
resent.

We must regulate our mind and body so we feel safe every
day,
and realize our love is sacred so we can express it in our
own way.

Work of Heart.

Compassion is our greatest spiritual power,
to show love to what is, both the sweet and the sour.

Love is to see ourselves in another,
to live like we all came from one Mother.

To forgive those who hurt us as they know not of their
sins,
they miss the mark of love, still counting their selfish wins.

Yet to realize they hurt themselves with every pain they
give,
Our love can help them see there's another way to live.

Forgiveness clears the mind and leaves room to create,
Humility loves all life and drowns out the hate.

By keeping the heart open we take back what is ours,
an unlimited source of love with all its Superpowers!

The Paradox.

A river can be flowing for many years,
yet the water remains so new.
In awareness we can realize a contradiction can still be true.
We know the Sun is very old, yet gives new warmth every
day,
and we can speak our truth with zero words we need to
say.
Sometimes we give people less by giving them more,
because our better self is being ground into the floor.
What if we feel our worst by always wanting our best,
and maybe the quickest route forwards is by having a rest.
Could it be that in wanting nothing, we gain everything?
Is it silence where heart begin to sing?
Perhaps in stillness we feel most moved,
By embracing chaos we live more soothed?
So what if we love what we once felt the need to hate?
Maybe anger and resentment will dissipate!
What if going into the dark is how we get to the light,
and could it be in complete surrender where we win the
fight?

Shoes.

If you were in their shoes you'd have done exactly the
same,
So think twice before throwing any hate or shame.

Our programming goes further back than our own Mam
and Dad,
Not many would consciously choose to be bad.

People who cause pain are hurting themselves too,
they can still be responsible without further ridicule from
me or you.

If we focus on blaming others or someone else's drama,
we give away our energy to something dealt with by Karma.

It's better to let things be, and not judge or assume,
Our attention is important and it starts with what we
consume!

Let's not compare to others, and make one of us win or
lose,
Love would always consider what it's like to be in their
shoes!

Compliments.

We don't reject a compliment because we are humble or
kind,
It's because it triggers the inadequacy we feel in our mind

Embrace that compliment and know it's what you deserve,
Don't shy away, play it down or swerve!

The more we are afraid to own any praise,
We're distancing from connection whatever someone says.

In addition we only feel hurt from criticism being threw,
If part of us believes deep down it is true!

We attract a love that matches the opinion of ourself,
so practice self-love like it's important for your health.

We are the generators for the experience we live,
and anything external we get to filter through our sieve.

We all have a story running in our mind,
It's not fixed in the past so choose one that's kind.

The Shadow.

The light side of us is what we show,
but we all have some dark that's hidden below,

What annoys us in others, is in ourselves too,
So when we are triggered let's see it as a clue.

Even our darkness can be channeled into good,
when we don't suppress it just to be understood.

If we grew up among anger it can make us exaggerate the kind,
but what bubbles below will blow the lid off your mind.

Once fully expressed no emotion is bad,
so integrate your darkness and stop resenting your Dad.

Aggression can be focused in a dance or some sports,
a much better release than fighting angry thoughts.

None of us are perfect, we're all capable of harm,
So loving our flaws will remove any alarm.

By integrating our whole self, there's no need for deceit,
Accept both light and dark knowing we're always complete!

Familiar.

We crave what's familiar even if that's bad,
Patterns run deep from the childhood we had,

We'll run from true love, because rejection feels
right,
We'll avoid feeling close because we're use to a
fight.

Take back your power, become aware how you
relate,
Don't let your subconscious turn into fate.

We're all a bit broken from a past that left scars,
but don't let it prison your heart behind bars!

All we want is safety, but we forget how it feels,
the past may be familiar, but it's the future that
heals

Engaged.

The whole world grows because of
conversation.
Whether you're English, American or Asian!
Societies are built on language and how we
relate.
The more personal the better, technology just
can't compensate!
Talking opens up possibilities,
be fully engaged, you'll see just what a thrill it
is!
Listening to another is not just with our ears,
We can experience their reality and feel their
fears!
Imagine giving someone the thought that you
truly know what they mean,
because there is no greater conversation than
one where you feel fully seen!

The Listener.

Imagine going your whole life without recognizing that you
never really listened to anyone,
You just listened to your own preconceived ideas, then you
blinked and their gone!

You heard you're own assumptions that you thought you
already knew,
While never hearing another and what they think is true!

Listening should be a sacred act,
an experience for both and not just attempting to dismantle
their fact.

Really hearing someone's story is a sign that we care,
Helping them relax into knowing we're really there!

Nobody knows the same person because of our projections
we all place,
So take a closer look at people and ask if you really know
beyond their face.

I'd rather.

I'd rather be happy than look happy,
I'd rather have one true friend than 50 who are
pretend.
I'd rather live in a rented flat but feel peace,
than live in a mansion yet never be at ease.
I'd rather give away true joy to many,
than competing with others for every penny.
I'd choose a life full of mistakes with lessons
learned,
Knowledge only becomes wisdom once it's earned.
I'd rather have the calm after a storm than no storm
at all,
Climbing high always feels better after a fall.
I'd rather have wrinkles than a flawless face,
and enjoy each step not seeing life as a race.
I'd rather feel seen by the love of my life,
than plan the perfect wedding just to call someone
my wife.
I'd rather sit with pain than avoid it with pleasure,
I'd rather feel good in my body without having to
measure.
I'd rather plant a seed than buy a tree,
I'd rather be flawed than perfect, so I'm loved for
me!

Progress.

Progress is when you no longer give mental space to the
things you once felt the need to control.
It's when you don't delay loving yourself until you reach a
goal.
Moving forwards is not thinking what you should have
done,
it's accepting you can only use energy from this day's sun.
Growth is knowing there's no rush to where you think you
oughta be,
because the present moment is the only place you can feel
free.
Improvement is feeling compassion when you once needed
to judge,
it's forgiveness when you'd previously hold a grudge.
Evolving isn't banishing your ego into the dark,
it's allowing all sides of you to play it's part.
To blossom is the awareness that's it's never about you,
so transcend into unity then love will come true!

Aligned.

My roots are in the ground, I am safe and I
know,
this is my journey of expression, leaving
footprints as I go.
What I create is my gift to give,
and to show that to love is the best way to
live.
From the pains of the dark I will grow strong
like a tree,
and I'll only ever speak what feels true to me.
My heart will remain kind and open for
connection,
and what I see in others will come from my
reflection.
Our bodies are expressions of a universal
soul,
We're individual drops of water, yet part of
the ocean as a whole.
We are miracles beyond our labels, not
defined by what's yours or mine,
Your energy is magic, you infinite, you are
Divine!

Tenderness.

I'm coming to believe that tenderness is the gateway
to oneness.
When we are tender towards things we are soft, we
are respectful in ways that are not rushed just to get
the task done.
Tenderness is a quiet loving presence, it doesn't
shout or seek praise. It's complete selflessness and
surrendering to a level of love and care beyond the
physical body.
Tenderness has no wants or desires, it is giving with
no motive other than to love what is now!
Tenderness cannot hurt another, for it doesn't see
another, it sees everything as one, it realizes we are
all drops from the same ocean.
Tenderness is one of loves greatest teachings, it is a
blanket of peace that you give to another that will
keep you both warm.
Try a little tenderness!

The Archetypes.

The path of the <u>Warrior</u> is the first journey you'll start,
Building the body, and making your mind smart.
Achieving your goals and putting a career in place,
But tame your ego, it's no competition or race.
The <u>Magician</u> is the next call you'll receive,
You'll learn beyond the physical and what happens when
you Believe!
Revealing what was hidden and shedding layers of your
past,
Entering realms beyond the body, once closed are now
vast!
It is the <u>Lover</u> who will give you the next call,
where you'll learn to open your heart and connect with one
and all.
You'll stop believing the past and calling things fate,
You're now fully present and ready to meet a soulmate.
The next call and the final one to ring,
is where you'll learn the values of the <u>Good King.</u>
You'll embody a leader, but not one with force,
you'll accept what is and let things run their course.
Your strength will be like water and be able to adapt,
with compassion you can now help others to feel less
trapped.
Before each call there was suffering, at times it felt like
Hell,
But it was all a necessary page in the story you can now
proudly tell,
What started as a struggle to understand your mental
health,
Was revealed as the journey back home to your true self.

Inner wisdom.

Being positive doesn't mean always walking with a
smile,
Maybe it's being ok carrying sadness for few mile.

Being strong doesn't mean fighting off all the stress,
it can be finding stillness in among the mess.

Just because you love, doesn't mean you should
keep,
It's better to let go if you'll finally get some sleep.

Sometimes the best message is the one that didn't
get sent,
better a pause than something that wasn't meant.

The answers we need are not always what we've
learnt,
Pain gives great wisdom but the feeling is where it's
earned.

Inner child.

There's a child inside me that hurts more than
I allow,
He whispers but I ignore him, yet when he
shouts I'm still wondering how.
I can heal him through listening and giving
him time to speak,
and by showing the root cause forgiveness
this doesn't make me weak.
Our inner child is in pain because he's
carrying all our past,
So offer him some kindness and the
reassurance it will last.
He gets anxious around any partners as he
thinks they won't understand,
because the little boy inside requests love as
his sole demand.

Break the chain.

Pain passed through generations hurts people today,
Carrying years of resentment thinking someone else
is to pay.

Anger deep inside means we can't truly live,
Yet freedom is so close if we just choose to forgive.

Compassion is a weapon that we can use against the
hate,
leaving room for connection and no need to
segregate.

We can heal ourselves with kindness from the
traumas of the past,
For a happier life today and relationships that will
last.

If the past is our heaviest burden and continues to
make us fall,
choose to open your heart,
and you'll realize Love does conquer all.

The passing.

The body may slip away, but the soul will remain,
In your heart, in stillness or as peace from any pain.

Just a meat suit expressing the universe through a
vehicle that walks,
But the Spirit is infinite and we'll feel it when it
talks.

Our mourning of the body is perfectly fine, a
necessary step in connecting to the Divine.

Then once we see that our tears will heal,
An essence stays with us that we will always feel.

Energy cannot die, so we'll always be around,
spreading love long after our body decays into the
ground.

Service.

Maybe we should give without wanting to receive,
Accept someone's truth without having to believe.

It's not all about us having to gain,
we can hold space for another while they sit with
their pain.

The gift in giving is the giving itself,
so maybe serving others can be good for our health.

Try listening to another without then wanting to
impress,
It's not all about you and your progress.

If you want to feel good without needing a flash
car,
help someone else, you'll see how important you
are!

Your life will add value the more that you give,
to be of service to others is the best way to live!

Where they are.

We're all on a journey, each on our own road,
It doesn't matter who is carrying the most load.

Some of us are spiritual, some like to compete,
Some are oblivious, yet don't even question if they are
complete.

Some of us read books, some of us just live,
some measure what they have by how much they give!

Some of us are doing the work, because all we want is to
heal,
So we can accept another's love now we know how to feel!

The wisest thing you've ever heard said,
could come from a homeless man who isn't well read!

There is no fixed path, or judgment on how far,
so let's love everyone exactly where they are!

Colour blind.

Two people can see the exact same thing in a different way
and both still be right, think about that the next time you
and your partner get into a fight.

Everyone is right from their point of view,
So not much can ever be factually true.

Someone may well be incorrect,
but that doesn't mean their feelings don't need respect.

Most people just want to have their word,
so they can be validated and feel heard.

So maybe it's not really about who's right or wrong,
and we can be on different hymn sheets but still singing the
same song!

By putting our egos aside and the need to settle a score,
We'll realize in togetherness that nothing matters more!

People pleaser.

Don't be someone that someone else wants you to be,
Don't fill up another's cup if it leaves yours empty!

Don't give all your energy if you get nothing back,
If you seek validation from others then you're in a state of
lack.

Better being hit by a truth, than kissed by a lie,
So stay true to yourself because time will soon fly.

Don't juggle plates to please everyone,
Many people may like you but you'll feel connected to
none.

We all want to be accepted, especially when life gets tough,
But remember that everything you have is already enough!

Life Goal.

I want the people I meet to feel a sense of
peace from me that when in my company
their nervous system immediately feels at ease
and safe so they can relax into the best
version of themselves.
I want people to feel zero judgment, and a
deep knowing that they can be vulnerable, and
express whatever comes up and it will be
received with love.

That's all!

Keep Loving.

Love doesn't separate or divide,
it's non-judgmental and it doesn't hide.

Love is unconditional and won't expect,
It's vulnerable and not striving to perfect!

Love isn't the loud success or end goal,
It's the unspoken daily watering of another's soul!

Love will always be our default state,
and only false stories we carry can make us hate.

We didn't come here to teach, we came here to
love,
but love is the greatest teacher, and makes
everything enough.

Love.

Love isn't a card from Moonpig, a Gucci belt or a
platinum ring,
It's something intangible inside us
and it makes the soul and heart sing!

We can love our friends and family
and be in love with our soulmate,
But there's also something much deeper,
and that kind doesn't segregate!

It is a love for all including yourself,
and it comes with no fear or judgment on wealth!
A limitless love, empty of conditions or desire,
We can start it through choice then it'll spread like
wildfire!

It can be used to heal and to end all war, and once
we feel it we'll stop searching for more!

Connection.

A drug we were born to crave, not let a
modern world treat us like a slave.
Eye contact, a smile, a chat about more than
the weather.
The real conversations that bring us together!
That warm fuzzy feeling sharing stories with a
lover, or being able to discuss each other's
faults openly with your Mother! Nights
around a campfire with a good friend, instead
of an Instagram life which is only pretend!
We can all find this chemistry and cherish this
connection,
and the world would have less pain and a lot
more affection.
It's what we really need, you can see it in our
faces,
If we realize this beauty in people aswell as in
places!

Attached.

How we connect with others can depend on how
we were raised.
Were we loved through touch, kind words or
praised?

Were our parents emotionally there, or did they buy
gifts to show they care?

We can be more self-aware by understanding our
past,
and build connections with those around us and
relationships that will last.

Secure, anxious, avoidant or too keen,
we all just want to be loved, heard and to be seen!

If you keep repeating a pattern that doesn't serve
you today,
Rewrite your story and love in your own way!

Sonder.

The realization that each random passerby is
living a life as vivid and as complex as your
own.
Even our deepest and most repetitive
thoughts we are not alone.
We all have our uniqueness in common
together,
and not just playing safe and making small
talk about the weather!
In a world of passing ships we are starved of
true connection,
let's share our vulnerability in exchange for
mutual affection!
We're a drop in the ocean, a mere flash in the
pan,
Let's love our weirdness before our course
has ran!

The Lonely crowd.

I can feel received without being heard,
I can be accepted without saying a word.
Someone can listen with more than their ears,
simply being there and understanding my fears.
I can also be greeted without feeling seen,
get a smile off someone that they don't really mean.
A true connection is more than going through the motions,
It's felt by the heart and it's deeper than all the oceans!
I can stand in a crowd yet still feel alone, stand solo on a mountain and it feel like my home.
In a world of passing ships and seeking validation through a phone,
it's your presence and attention that will stop people feeling alone!

Dear Mam,

"This world isn't what you promised,
everywhere I look is pain.
You said it'd be full of sunshine,
but I'm just sheltering from the rain!
You promised a life of happiness,
and every day would be one of joy!
But this world is hurting me,
forcing me to consume or destroy!"

Dear Son,

"You have to see the whole world, not be hidden from its
flaws.
You need tough times to help you grow,
so don't be defeated by their cause!
Look closer and you'll see the joys each day, and realize we
all have cracks but that the light gets in this way!
You aren't entitled to zero pain or good times that forever
last!
Remember it's not what you see it's the way you see it that
gives beauty to life's contrast!

Relationships.

Our relationships form the backbone of society. If we get them right then most other things will fall into place. One of the highest forms of human happiness and fulfilment is due to our bond and connection with others, we are social creatures and happiness is multiplied when it is shared. Have you ever noticed that when your relationship at home is suffering you will struggle being present at work, and if your relationship with your work colleagues is struggling then you won't be present at home. Like anything worth having, relationships take work, compromise and sacrifice.

Be it your boss, colleagues, friends, family or lover, compassion is the foundation of any relationship. We live in a time where relationships are seen more and more as transactional exchanges; with the main stance of "what am I getting out of this?" Which leads to a lack of presence, only listening to respond and seeing the relationship as a means to an end! The paradox here being that in order to feel a true deep connection which really brings a relationship to life, you have to be fully present, listen attentively and flow with it selflessly with no hidden motives.

There is literally a hormone that gets released when we feel connected to others called oxytocin, which is a known pain killer and makes us happy. This year has been tough, with divides in opinions over black, white, vaccine, no vaccine, in or out. So we need to cherish our relationships, work at them and feed them because they affect everything we do. By doing so we can make our own lives and those around us so much better!

Feelings.

Still your mind and open your heart
before your relationships go past the start.

Don't carry your hurt from place to place,
so that the people you meet can see beyond
your face!

Compassion and time should be your first
meal,
In order to set intentions and allow yourself
to heal

Honour your tears and don't lock emotions in
a jar
Be free and love yourself for all that you are!

The Best of You.

I wonder how many beautiful pieces of art Netflix and chills has robbed from us? Potential that has remained untapped due to us selecting the easier option over sitting with a pen and paper.

How many magical conversations have been missed due to mindlessly phone scrolling and avoiding that longing for connection in the eyes of others. I'm coming to realize that these easy choices may come from a desire for peace from their own mind, an escapism from their own thoughts. The quick dopamine hit from Instagram and the evening Netflix binge are surely now regarded as the less angry cousins of alcohol and drugs. But they should certainly not be dismissed lightly. Of course, both perfectly fine in moderation, but can cause havoc if they are to the detriment of such things like; connecting with others over real conversation, doing something creative or even just ensuring you have periods of being fully present in your day. I believe these things are imperative to a fulfilled life, where we aren't looking to escape or numb that mild hum of anxiety through instant pleasure. Think about how uplifted you feel after a great conversation, feeling heard and engaging on a deeper than surface level is really quite healing for the human soul. Think about how time is of no importance when you are fully encapsulated in learning a new skill or doing something creative like writing, drawing or even dancing for that matter. The answers are simple if we just care enough to find them, and we can actually live our lives in true peace if we realize that the key is just to fully engage in the means and not be fixed on the pleasure at the ends. The next conversation you have, or even the next dog walk or making a cup of tea, do yourself a favour and be fully present for it. You may think it's silly until you experience the levels of peace on offer when you fully commit to the present moment. Lately my sense of joy is being less derived from an outside stimulus, any more things like; noticing the level of detail in the bark or a tree, watching and listening to the sound of my dog drink from a river, noticing subtle facial expressions of my girlfriend when we talk about something she's excited by, comparing clouds to paintings. I now really believe that by giving everything the best of you, you'll be gifted with the best of life.

Please me.

Don't be someone that someone else wants you to
be,
Don't fill up another's cup if it leaves yours empty!

Don't give all your energy if you get nothing back,
If you seek validation from others then you're in a
state of lack.

Better being hit by a truth, than kissed by a lie,
So stay true to yourself because time will soon fly.

Don't juggle plates to please everyone,
Many people may like you but you'll feel connected
to none.

We all want to be accepted, especially when life gets
tough,
But remember that everything you have is already
enough!

Happy Me ever after.

We all crave our happily ever after, that love story worthy
of a bafta.

We'll force a square peg in a round hole,
Just to have someone to share the leading role.

We cannot heal others to get more intimacy under the
covers.
Trying to fix people will tear you apart, leaving nothing but
a broken heart.

Failed relationships will make us question ourself,
as we seek from the pages of others, what we can find on
our own book shelf.

What we need we start to impede,
but what we let be will grow like a tree!

Be your own love story, and then love will find you,
a kind felt by the heart and you'll know that it's true.

Penny for a thought.

I people watch from coffee shops and wonder what life
they live,
Is that resting bitch face just a decoy for all the kindness
they give?

I'm an extroverted introvert who can be confident in a
crowd,
But then I need time in nature away from anything that's
loud.

I want to connect with everyone but I love being alone,
My door is always open but I'm normally the only one
home.

I read a chapter of a book each day,
Not to be smart, just to have something to say.
I work my body to look strong and tough,
Or is it because I want to feel like I'm enough?

I suppose we'll never know anyone, unless we're inside
their head,
These are just some thoughts of mine, and now I'm going
to bed!

5. Nature's medicine.

Wild Peace.

When I can't escape the thoughts of
tomorrow,
or I'm trapped in uncertainty with
undertones of sorrow,
I head to the forest where the conifer
trees grow,
In the presence of their stillness my mind
starts to slow.
Musical syllables of the skylark are
increasingly near,
the Birdsong becomes a remedy to
dissolve all my fear.
My senses are heightened, no separation
from nature and me,
If just for a moment I'm limitlessly free!

Re-Wild.

Going back to what feels right,
take off those shoes you've been wearing
too tight!
Feel the rhythm of the forest, this is
where we're meant to be,
Let go of any stresses and start to feel
free!
Breathe in the air of the wild,
be playful and dance just like a child.
In nature there's no judgment or
comparison of wealth.
What matters most is connection and
walking each other home to our true self!

Birthright.

Let go of the social constraints of what it means to
be a woman or a man,
It's time to remember what it means to be a human

No expectations are held so let these go from your
mind,
Let judgments slip away and allow space to be
compassionate and kind

Take a deep sigh and fully release what you've been
suppressing,
let all energy flow and start expressing.

Have faith in the magic and miracles will start
growing,
the belief of what's possible will now be a deep
knowing!

Reclaim your birthright and take charge of your
health,
and in the connection to others you'll realise your
true self!

Human, Nature.

Nature is never in order but somehow not a
mess,
it's not striving for perfection, yet we don't
see it any less!
We don't criticise the mountains for not
standing in a row,
or cast judgment on the valleys when they are
low.
We don't blame the stars or question how
they scatter,
and tree branches grow in all directions but
somehow it doesn't matter.
Clouds don't make continuous patterns of
four,
Yet we're accepting and don't expect anything
more.
Nature will give but it will also take,
It's untrustworthy but it's never a mistake.
We can always tolerate what nature does,
Let's take this as a lesson because Nature is
Us!

At one with nature.

Nature is calming because it connects us to
who we are,
We are part of the universe just like a star!

We did not come "into" this world
We came "out of" this world!
It is not "the" planet, it's "your" planet.
It is not "the" trees it's "our" trees!
If we change how we see we can live life with
ease!
Change is pain, but pain is growth,
So don't hold on, just surrender to what is
and flow!

If you think you are big, you become small,
If you know you are nothing you'll be
limitlessly tall.
The sky is never ending, a tree doesn't give a
shit about the news,
So remember your power and there's nothing
you can lose!

Back to our roots.

We're just educated apes living on a rock we call earth, so let's milk the fuck out of life for all that it's worth! Dance in the forest, camp on the hill, shout random words in the shower it'll give you a thrill!
Close your eyes and smile, take a deep breath and just sit there a while! Read The Gruffalo's child and Where the wild things are, view the bigger picture, you are literally a star! Choose a simple life, don't just work to buy a car, pass this message to your kids and they'll be sure to go far!
Smile more and know the importance of eye contact and touch, the little things that truly mean much! Be thankful and enjoy your food, sing in the car, it'll change your mood! Tell stories, work up a sweat, ask more questions, who knows what you'll get! Throw stones in the river, watch the stars, talk about movies and wonder what it's like to live on mars!
Tell Dad jokes, slow down and don't hurry, make time for your Nana and remember not to worry! Don't seek love, be love, create more than you consume, tell the truth, and for kindness always make room!
Get to know yourself, meditate, take pride in making your bed, enjoy today because one day you'll be dead!
Experience new things, open your mind, don't settle, find a romantic lover, then life's magical little things you'll find in each other!
Get out of your own way, see the world like a child, get back to your roots, be free and be wild!
The things that count can't be counted, you don't need to think how. Chase moments of awe that will face slap you into the now!
Expect less, appreciate more and you can't go wrong! We spend our lives searching only to realise what we needed was within us all along!

Live wild.

Nature is waiting, so get out and explore,

Mother Nature has medicine, she will heal and restore!

Seek adventure, be free, see the world like a child,

Life can be magic, if you choose to live wild!

Spring into life.

A new beginning as the ice starts to thaw,
lambs full of life and bluebells carpet the
floor,

A chance to start over, let old habits go,
appreciate life's cycles and watch new beauty
grow!

With nature comes balance, from death to
rebirth,
The sun will get warmer as life blossoms from
the earth

There's a lesson we can take for every season
that arrives,
after the dark of winter, we appreciate light
with fresh eyes!

I am a wild swimmer,

At home in any lake or sea!
A post hike dip on a sunny day,
or running into the waves when the sky is
grey!
Jumping in a tarn surrounded by trees
and moonlit swims when the lake is about to
freeze!
Whatever the day may bring, it's made better
after a wild swim!
When immersed in the water all my worries
disappear,
I'm connected to nature without a single fear!
I am a wild swimmer, I feel so alive and free,
and my favourite swims are the ones shared
with friends, topped off with a flask of tea!

The Wild Camper.

The freedom of having everything you need
in a backpack, and off you go.
Once pitched up, we just take it slow!
Back to your roots, among nature and the
stars, away from the rat race or roads full of
cars!
There's no competing or running to get
somewhere,
with a sky full of magic, we just sit there and
stare!
Deeper conversation with a sunset view, then
drifting off to sleep under a shooting star or 2!
Nothing beats that sound of a tent unzipping
to reveal the beautiful light of dawn,
then a brew and back down feeling like you've
been reborn!

The Fall.

Those fresh, crisp mornings will soon be here.
The orange and brown leaves show change is
nothing to fear!

Watch the steam arise from your coffee cup,
as you gaze at the autumnal mountains you'll soon
head up.

Adventures in the fells, then the comfort food we'll
earn,
followed by cozy nights listening to a log fire burn.

A daily reminder to playfully kick the leaves, stop to
appreciate the colours, and that it's ok to fall.
I think Autumn is my favourite season of all

Hurry less.

A tree grows strong from its roots
underneath,
yet it doesn't need to shout, it just stands
still in peace!

Flowers never speak, yet can speak to our
hearts,
by sitting in a garden we can see how
beauty starts!

The sun warms us daily, yet rises very
slow,
it takes its time to set, but makes all
below it grow!

We don't have to race like we're
competing in a run,
Nature never hurries yet everything gets
done!

Alive the most.

The second you face your fear you become
fully free,
You are now in control of a new limitless
energy!
Our fears can be a source of power,
let them awaken your soul,
Get comfortable being uncomfortable and
make it a daily goal!
There's a place of pure presence, and where
you'll feel most at home,
It's not far to get to, but it's beyond your
comfort zone!
Lean into adversity and pain, don't run and
hide,
this life is for living on the edge and enjoying
the ride!
It's easy scrolling Instagram and being warm
as toast,
but try a dip in some ice cold water,
then see which makes you feel alive the most!

The Lakeland fells.

Start on the ground in the woodland trails,
heading for the natural highs
facing sun, rain or gales!
Flowing rivers, eerie tarns and deep ravines,
A blissful adventure
where the soul sings and the heart gleams,
It's just the mountain and you
and if you conquer adversity
you can appreciate the view,
The soothing smells, the calming sounds,
The beautiful Lakeland fells,
where we can lose our minds
and find ourselves!

Who am I?

Am I the name given to me at birth,
or is this just a label that carries no real worth?

Am I the thoughts going round in my head,
or the dreams I have when asleep in my bed?

Am I my face of which others see and know,
or am I something else, something deeper below?

Am I the job that I do every day,
or is this just a time filler that helps me get pay?

Maybe I'm the hobbies or what I post online,
but these seem too external and finite of time.

I believe I'm the energy, which is boundless and free,
and I share this with everything from a human to a tree!

I am the conscious awareness that connects us all as one,
which will continue to live long after my body is gone!

The magic in my soul can't be seen by the eye,
It's a knowing that it's there like the stars in the sky.

If we think we are separate, we will destroy or divide,
So remember we are one then love cannot hide!

Stillness.

The mind is turning like an out of control hamster
wheel,
worrying about a future that isn't even real.

We are constantly moving or obsessing on the past,
rarely being present and making this moment last.

Nature is our best teacher, just look at a tree,
the same stillness and calm can be found in you are
me.

So don't walk for your dog or just to burn your next
pound,
Really notice what you see, because that's where
true peace is found.

Life can be busy and make us feel stressed,
but nature gives us freedom where we can only feel
blessed!

The Elements.

Disconnected to ourselves, because we've lost
touch with the earth,
walk barefoot and feel grounded,
You'll soon see what it's worth.

Camp around a fire and watch the embers glow,
your problems are non-existent around nature's
firework show.

Feel limitless in water as you swim wild and free,
like a child for the first time, you are starting to see.

Breathe deeply to gain power, so in stressful times
you'll thrive,
these connections with nature show us what it
means to be alive

The Wisdom of Waterfalls.

They have power and persistence
one of nature's greatest shows!
Resilience and calm in the way their water
flows!

A continuous symphony totally free of charge,
and a visual beauty in both little ones and
large!

Good days or bad, they will never completely
hide,
and any facing obstacle they take swiftly in
their stride!

Through simply observing nature
we can learn to carry on through it all
and realise it's ok to fall!

The Mountain.

A symbol of achievement, conquering and
getting to the top,
everlasting, resilient and refusing to stop!
Always changing, yet constant beauty, as each
season will show.
Majestic in nature, but still humble as the trees
below.
A mountain of wisdom or a metaphor for life,
or simply a nice view on a Sunday stroll with
the wife.
Peak bagger, Wainwright ticker,
or wild camper watching the stars flicker.
Born from an ice age, and still standing tall,
the mountain is magic and has something for
us all!

Win the morning!

Alarm goes off, it's dark outside.
The voice in my head wants me to hide!
But then I remember the joy of last time,
which makes the internal voice a mere
distant twine!
Jumping in the sea to feel alive,
there's no better way!
And when you win the morning, you also
win the day!

Hidden Joy.

One man walks alone into the sea.
It's 6am and I know where I'd rather be.
But sometimes the joys are hidden beyond
what we can see, for sustained happiness
discipline is the key.

Everything you own will one day be thrown away, or at best stashed away and kept in a loft. The only thing that lives on is the impact you have had on others.

Favourite quotes.

"It is by logic that we prove, but by intuition that we discover."

"We don't see things as they are, we see things as we are"

"Kiss the joy and let it fly, you'll enjoy life more knowing one day you'll die"

"Expect nothing, appreciate everything"

"If you are not happy with a coffee you won't be happy with a yacht"

"No rain, no flowers!"

"Don't wish for an easy life, wish for the strength to endure a difficult one."

"We shouldn't try to fix everything that comes into in our lives, just fix ourselves so that whatever comes along we'll will be fine!"

"We didn't come here to teach we came to love, and love is the best teacher."

Printed in Great Britain
by Amazon

14522125R00119